COLLECTOR'S VALUE GUIDE

Harry Potter Collectibles

Collector Handbook and Price Guide

PREMIERE EDITION

Harry Potter Collectibles

The Collector's Value Guide™ is not sponsored or endorsed by, or otherwise affiliated with J. K. Rowling, Warner Bros. or its licensees. Harry Potter is a trademark owned by Time Warner Entertainment Company, L.P. CheckerBee Publishing is not associated with this trademark. Any opinions expressed are solely those of the authors, and do not necessarily reflect those of J. K. Rowling, Warner Bros. or its licensees. Special thanks to Alan Wheal.

Front cover (left to right): Foreground – "Norbert With Egg" – Kurt S. Adler,
"Hermione" – Enesco
Background – "Harry Potter™ Harry And Hagrid™ At Gringotts™"
– Department 56®, "Quidditch™ Pen/Paper Gift Set" – Hallmark

Back cover (left to right): "Hedwig™ The Owl" – Department 56®,
"Professor Dumbledore™" – Hallmark

EDITORIAL
Managing Editor: Jeff Mahony
Associate Editors: Melissa A. Bennett
Jan Cronan
Gia C. Manalio
Mike Micciulla
Paula Stuckart
Assistant Editors: Heather N. Carreiro
Jennifer Filipek
Joan C. Wheal
Editorial Assistants: Timothy R. Affleck
Beth Hackett
Christina M. Sette
Steven Shinkaruk

WEB
(CollectorsQuest.com)
Web Reporter: Samantha Bouffard
Web Graphic Designer: Ryan Falis

PRODUCTION
Production Manager: Scott Sierakowski

ART
Creative Director: Joe T. Nguyen
Assistant Art Director: Lance Doyle
Senior Graphic Designers: Marla B. Gladstone
Susannah C. Judd
David S. Maloney
Carole Mattia-Slater
David Ten Eyck
Graphic Designers: Jennifer J. Bennett
Sean-Ryan Dudley
Kimberly Eastman
Melani Gonzalez
Caryn Johnson
Jaime Josephiac
Jim MacLeod
Jeremy Maendel
Chery-Ann Poudrier
Angi Shearstone

R&D
Priscilla Berthiaume
Amy Kusiak
Paul Rasid

ISBN 1-58598-073-0

CHECKERBEE™ and COLLECTOR'S VALUE GUIDE™ are trademarks of CheckerBee, Inc. Copyright © 2000 by CheckerBee, Inc.
All rights reserved. No part of this book may be reproduced or transmitted in any form or by any means, electronic or mechanical, including photocopying, recording, or by any information storage or retrieval system, without the written permission of the publisher.

CheckerBee PUBLISHING
306 Industrial Park Road
Middletown, CT 06457

CollectorsQuest.com

TABLE OF CONTENTS

Introducing The Collector's Value Guide™ • 5

Wizardry And Witchcraft Through The Ages • 6

The Magic All Around Us • 9

Harry Potter Reader's Checklist • 15

Collecting Harry Potter • 21

Harry Potter In The Headlines • 25

Harry Potter Enchants The World Wide Web • 35

Around The Globe With Harry Potter • 40

Harry Potter In The Schools • 44

J. K. Rowling: A Wizard Of Words • 47

A Portrait Of The Artists • 55

Harry Potter Product Showcase • 59

    The First Years • 59

    Warner Bros. Product Spotlight • 63

    A Magical Challenge • 81

    A Wizard's Wardrobe • 86

    Back To School • 92

    Through The Picture Frame • 96

    The Neverending Feast • 101

Table Of Contents

How To Use Your Collector's Value Guide™ • 104

Value Guide – Harry Potter • 105

    The Books • 105

    International Books • 111

Collectibles Showcase • 119

    Department 56® • 119

    Enesco • 121

    Kurt S. Adler • 126

    Hallmark • 133

Harry Potter Product Diary • 144

Total Value Of My Collection • 161

A Wizard's Guide To The Secondary Market • 163

Map Of Great Britain • 166

Journey With Harry Through England • 168

What's Cooking In The Cauldron?! • 177

Fun Facts • 182

Magic Words • 187

If You Like Harry Potter, Try . . . • 189

INTRODUCING THE COLLECTOR'S VALUE GUIDE™

Welcome to the premiere edition of the Collector's Value Guide™ to Harry Potter Collectibles. In 1997, the first of the Harry Potter series of children's books began a craze which would travel (as if by magic broomstick) from the shores of Great Britain to the United States and, eventually, to almost every corner of the globe. Today, Harry Potter has amassed a tremendous following of fans of all ages who are enchanted with his world of mystical mayhem.

The Value Guide is a great way to harness some of the power of the Harry Potter phenomena. In its pages you will find a showcase of all of the Harry Potter products that will be offered by officially licensed companies. Next, you'll find a complete listing of the American and British books, along with secondary market values, as well as a section spotlighting books available in foreign languages. And that's just the beginning! In this book, you will also find:

* **Color photos of the American, British and international book covers**
* **A spotlight on Harry Potter collectibles**
* **News headlines from the world of Harry Potter**
* **An entertaining look at English culture**
* **Quirky recipes, fun facts and a glossary of magic words**
* **Plus much, much more!**

Wizardry And Witchcraft Through The Ages

J. K. Rowling's Harry Potter books are filled with magical creatures, mysterious spells and powerful wizards – subjects that have fascinated humans since the beginning of time. Stories of witches and wizards can be found in folk and fairy tales, legends and myths. Originally, they were passed through story telling and later written down. Here's a look at some legendary witches and wizards who could rival even Professor Dumbledore.

Magic And The Rise Of Science

Wizards have been around since the beginning of time and were important figures in the ancient world. They played many roles such as priests, astrologists, court magicians and diviners and indeed, Harry Potter would be proud to take his place among them.

One such famous wizard was Merlin, a Welsh magician who played an important part in the birth of King Arthur (of Round Table fame). Merlin eventually became Arthur's friend, confidante and magician and has gone down in history as one of the greatest wizards of all time.

In the Middle Ages, a new art came to Europe from Arabia known as alchemy. Alchemy is commonly known as the practice of turning metal into gold, but this goal is only part of a larger search. The transformation of metal into gold was

thought to make the alchemist's spirit completely pure. As a result, an alchemist who learned to turn metal into gold would have the power to live forever!

In order to achieve his goals, an alchemist needed the Philosopher's Stone, which readers will recognize from *Harry Potter and the Philosopher's Stone* (or *Sorcerer's Stone* as it is titled in the United States). This mystical substance would lead to immortality as it would stop the aging process and cure all diseases. No wonder Lord Voldemort wanted to find it so badly!

Paracelsus and Nicholas Flamel are two alchemists whose names (readers of the Harry Potter series will recognize) are closely tied to the Philosopher's Stone. Paracelsus is said to have produced the Philosopher's Stone and an elixir of life. Nicholas Flamel translated a manuscript which contained clues to the transformation of metal. Flamel is thought to have produced gold, with which he made generous donations to hospitals and churches. Since he had possession of the Philosopher's Stone, many believe that he and his wife – who helped him with his work – are still alive.

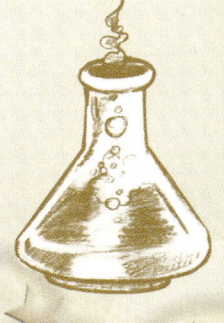

WITCHES IN HISTORY

Witches have existed for untold ages. They began as spiritual figures or priestesses. However, during the medieval period, the label "witch" gained a negative connotation. Much like the Animagus in Harry's world, it was believed that witches could change their shape into that of an animal and travel undetected to cause mischief. Witches were also thought to be able to control the weather. Perhaps most frightening was the Evil Eye. It was believed that witches who possessed this ability had only to gaze at a person and illness and bad luck would follow.

Today, there is a form of witchcraft called Wicca. Practitioners of Wicca celebrate the power of nature and pride themselves on doing good deeds. These modern day witches are a unified group, often coming together at festivals on particular occasions throughout the year, where they sing, dance and enjoy the company of friends and family.

Harry Potter is sure to have learned about all of these legendary wizards, alchemists and practices in Professor Binns' "History of Magic" class. And these studies are sure to have helped him understand his role within the wizard community.

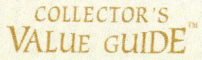

The Magic All Around Us

Now that you've learned a little bit about real wizards and witches from history, let's take a look at how magic, wizardry and witchcraft has been portrayed in popular culture through the years. Magic and sorcery has always been a point of fascination for humans, but the way that we have viewed the supernatural has changed over time. With the debut of the movie *Harry Potter and the Sorcerer's Stone* in 2001, Harry Potter will become the latest in a long line of wizards and witches to hit the silver screen. Here's a look at some other famous witches, wizards and sorcerers who have found fame through books, television and film over the years.

Books

Long before the character of Harry Potter came to life in the 1990s, another English wizard found literary fame. **Merlin**, best known for his role in the Arthurian legends, is the subject of several books. According to folklore, Merlin arranged the "sword-in-the-stone" contest which enabled Arthur to become the king of England.

Although the three witches in William Shakespeare's tragedy, **Macbeth,** have a small role, they make prophecies about

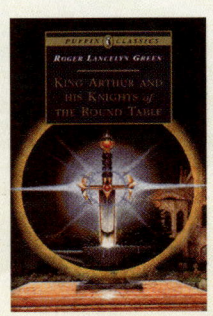

The cover of *King Arthur and his Knights of the Round Table* by Roger Lancelyn Green.

Macbeth's future that may have affected his actions later in the story. Summoning their skills in divination, the witches in this book are heard chanting, "Double, double toil and trouble; Fire burn, and cauldron bubble . . .".

The Lion, The Witch and The Wardrobe is the second book in *The Chronicles of Narnia* series. In this tale, four British children find a secret passageway in a closet to the magical land of Narnia. They befriend a lion and the group works together to restore beauty to Narnia when the White Witch casts a spell of perpetual winter.

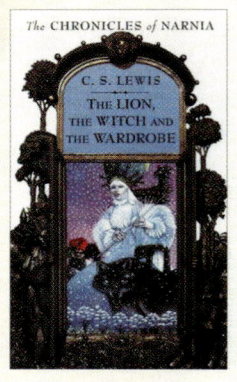
The cover of *The Lion, The Witch and The Wardrobe.*

The Witches is a classic book by children's author Roald Dahl in which a 7-year-old boy finds out the truth about witches when he is trapped in a room filled with them while on vacation with his grandmother. The boy learns that witches use wigs and makeup to disguise themselves as average-looking women, making it very difficult to identify them! As he learns everything he ever wanted to know about witches (including their appetite for little boys and girls!), the boy uncovers a plot to harm all of the children in Great Britain.

The cover of *The Witches* by Roald Dahl.

TELEVISION

The 1960s television show **Bewitched** prompted girls all around the country to wiggle their noses and try to cast spells. Samantha, the show's main character, is a perky blond housewife who is also a witch. She uses her spells to get herself and her mortal husband, Darrin, out of (and into!) all sorts of comical situations. Add a meddling mother-in-law, a nosy neighbor and assorted warlocks and spells, and you get a popular sitcom that remained on the air for eight seasons.

Beginning its third year on the WB network, **Charmed**, a television show starring actresses Shannen Doherty, Alyssa Milano and Holly Marie Combs, focuses on three 20-something sisters who discover that they are witches. Each girl has been blessed with her own special power: one can move things with her mind, one can freeze time and one can see into the future. The girls attempt to adjust to their new-found identities as they fight wicked warlocks and other evil spirits.

On The Radio

Sorcery has not only made a splash in books, television and film – it has also been the subject for a number of songs throughout history. Here are a few of our favorites:

"Pinball Wizard"
The Who

"Witch Doctor"
Various

"Witchcraft"
Elvis Presley

"Witchy Woman"
The Eagles

Sabrina, the Teenage Witch, a weekly television program which aired on the ABC network until the Fall of 2000 when it moved to WB, features actress Melissa Joan Hart as a modern teenage witch who is just learning to use her magical powers with the help of her two aunts, with whom she lives. Sabrina often ends up using her magic the wrong way, which leads to some strange situations!

While Sabrina does not fit the typical stereotype of a witch, she does have a black cat named Salem. Salem, who was named after the famous Salem Witch Trials in Massachusetts, often gives Sabrina advice in difficult situations and provides comic relief on the show.

Film

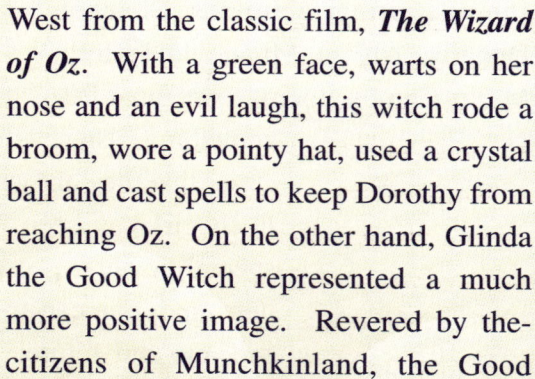

When most people think of the term "witch," they think of the image of the Wicked Witch of the West from the classic film, ***The Wizard of Oz***. With a green face, warts on her nose and an evil laugh, this witch rode a broom, wore a pointy hat, used a crystal ball and cast spells to keep Dorothy from reaching Oz. On the other hand, Glinda the Good Witch represented a much more positive image. Revered by the citizens of Munchkinland, the Good Witch travels in a bubble, has a gentle attitude and always looks beautiful. The film also featured the Wonderful Wizard of Oz, a powerful wizard who gave Dorothy the secret to getting home. While the wizard at first seemed powerful and intimidating, he really turned out to be a kind, old man.

A boy named Bastian finds a book called **The NeverEnding Story** and soon is drawn in by its tale of fantasy, witches and warriors. It focuses on a land called Fantasia, which has been created by the fantasies of readers. As Bastian becomes engrossed in the story, he realizes that it is his fate to join the magical creatures of Fantasia and save the land from the Nothingness that threatens to destroy it.

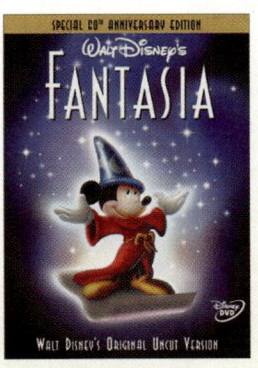

A sorcerer appears on the cover of the *Fantasia* video.

The 1940 classic animated Walt Disney film **Fantasia** portrayed the lovable Mickey Mouse as an apprentice to a sorcerer who, with the help of a wand, a cauldron and some classical music, conjures up plenty of magic. Unicorns and other mythological creatures can also be seen in the film, as well as a recap of the creation of the world and dancing animals.

Several Disney movies focus on the struggle between good and evil, often using witches as the source of evil. **Sleeping Beauty** featured the evil witch Maleficent, who attempts to kill

Dream Team

In the course of the Harry Potter books, we discover that Ron Weasley's favorite Quidditch team is the Chudley Cannons. However, for Harry Potter fans who prefer basketball, the ultimate dream game might consist of a match-up between the NBA's Washington Wizards and the Orlando Magic!

our heroine Princess Aurora with a poisonous spinning wheel before she turns 16.

Disney also produced the film **Teen Witch**, about an unpopular girl named Louise who learns that she is the descendant of witches. Louise uses her powers to get revenge on her enemies, while gaining popularity and the affection of the captain of the football team.

Hocus Pocus is a comedy about three witches from the age of the Salem Witch Trials (played by Bette Midler, Sarah Jessica Parker and Kathy Najimy) who were accidentally conjured into modern-day Salem as a result of a child's Halloween prank. The witches, who keep busy flying around on vacuum cleaners and tormenting trick-or-treaters, are determined to find immortality and it's up to a group of children and an enchanted cat to stop them.

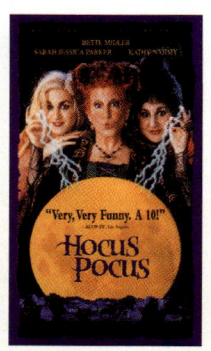

The cover of *Hocus Pocus* videocassette, depicting the three popular stars.

These are just a few examples of the many roles that sorcery has assumed in our culture through the years. In addition to the stories about witches and wizards, our society is filled with tales of ghosts, dragons and mythological creatures just like those found in the halls of Hogwarts Castle!

Harry Potter Reader's Checklist

With over 30 translations available in over 100 countries, the series of books about a wizard orphan named Harry Potter has captured the hearts and imaginations of children around the world. It has inspired a return to the hobby of reading that, in this age of television and video games, was thought to be extinct. Even adults have been captivated by the story of Harry and his friends. Written with universal charm and humor, the books appeal to readers of all ages. Everyone can relate to the tale of a boy who gets to escape his dreary existence and live a life of magic. If only it could happen to us!

You can tell by looking at this Enesco bookend that Hermione has always known how much fun it is to read a good book.

In the first book of the series, 11-year-old Harry Potter learns that he is a wizard and will be attending the Hogwarts School of Witchcraft and Wizardry. There, Harry discovers many new things about his past and his talents, his family, his friends and his dangerous enemies. During the next four years, Harry works toward his goal of becoming a wizard his parents would have been proud of!

This section will help you keep track of your reading adventures with Harry Potter, as author J. K. Rowling has now published four books in what will be a seven-book series. The publication information is for the United States hardcover editions.

Harry Potter Reader's Checklist

☐ I Read It!

HARRY POTTER
AND THE SORCERER'S STONE

OCTOBER 1998 • SCHOLASTIC PRESS • 309 PAGES

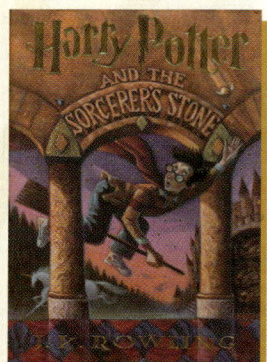

The cover of Book 1 features Harry flying on a broomstick.

Harry Potter enters his first year at Hogwarts School and, with his new friends, Ron Weasley and Hermione Granger, he discovers secrets that have been locked away for years. The trio of friends encounter devious classmates, suspicious professors and magical creatures all before stumbling upon the most dangerous enemy!

DATE READ: _____

MY RATING (CIRCLE): ★ ★ ★ ★ ★

MY COMMENTS: _____
_____
_____

U.S. Awards, 1998:

* *Booklist* – Editors' Choice
* *Publishers Weekly* – Best Book of the Year
* *School Library Journal* – Best Book of the Year

New York Times #1 Over 90 Weeks On List

U.S. Awards, 1999:

*American Library Association –
   Notable Children's Book, Best Book for Young Adults

U.K. Awards, 1997:

* British Book Awards – Children's Book of the Year
* The Federation of Children's Book Groups – Children's Book Award
* Nestlé Smarties Book Prize – Gold Medal

COLLECTOR'S VALUE GUIDE™

☐ I Read It!

HARRY POTTER
AND THE CHAMBER OF SECRETS

JUNE 1999 • SCHOLASTIC PRESS • 341 PAGES

Harry Potter
AND THE
CHAMBER
OF SECRETS
On the cover of Book 2, Harry is again caught in mid-flight.

Harry endures another summer with the Dursleys and is looking forward to returning to school. Just before the start of the school year, he is given an ominous warning to stay away from Hogwarts. But brave Harry returns to the school to deal with loads of schoolwork, a pretentious new teacher and a whole new mystery!

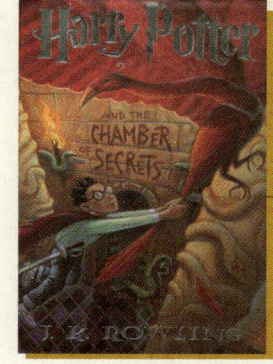

DATE READ: ________________________

MY RATING (CIRCLE): ★ ★ ★ ★ ★

MY COMMENTS: ____

____

____

New York Times #1
Over 60 Weeks On List

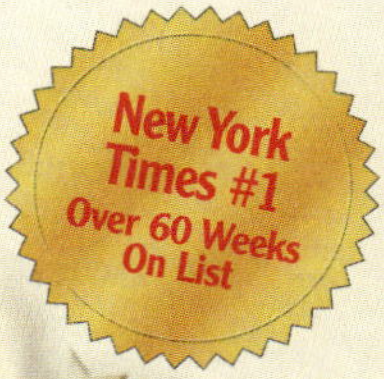

U.S. Awards, 1999:

* *Publishers Weekly* – Best Book of the Year
* *School Library Journal* – Best Book of the Year

U.K. Awards, 1998:

* British Book Awards – Children's Book of the Year
* The Federation of Children's Book Groups – Children's Book Award
* Nestlé Smarties Book Prize – Gold Medal

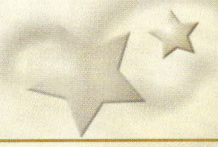

Harry Potter and the Prisoner of Azkaban

 I Read It!

October 1999 • Scholastic Press • 435 pages

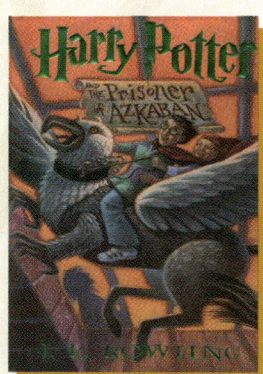

The cover of Book 3 features Harry and Hermione.

A prisoner has escaped and the Ministry of Magic suspects he's out to kill Harry Potter. Harry spends his third year at Hogwarts living in fear, both of the dangerous escapee and of the soul-sucking, hooded creatures known as dementors that have been dispatched to track the prisoner down.

Date Read: _____

My Rating (circle): ★ ★ ★ ★ ★

My Comments: _____
_____
_____

U.S. Awards, 1999:

* *Booklist* – Editors' Choice
* *Publishers Weekly* – Best Book of the Year

New York Times #1 Over 50 Weeks On List

U.K. Awards, 1999:

* British Book Awards – Author of the Year
* The Federation of Children's Book Groups – Children's Book Award

I Read It!

HARRY POTTER
AND THE GOBLET OF FIRE

JULY 2000 • SCHOLASTIC PRESS • 734 PAGES

During the Triwizard Tournament held at Hogwarts, Harry Potter battles through scandals, dangerous tasks and tragedies. Meanwhile, the appearance of an ominous symbol in the sky at the Quidditch World Cup leads to speculation that Harry's greatest "competitor" of all is getting stronger and the reign of terror will resume.

The cover of Book 4 features a close-up of Harry.

DATE READ: _____

MY RATING (CIRCLE): ★ ★ ★ ★ ★

MY COMMENTS:_____
_____
_____

New York Times #1 Over 10 Weeks On List

Harry Potter Reader's Checklist

☐ Book 5:
I Read It!

SUMMARY:_____
_____
_____

DATE READ:_____
MY RATING (CIRCLE): ★ ★ ★ ★ ★
MY COMMENTS:_____
_____

☐ Book 6:
I Read It!

SUMMARY:_____
_____
_____

DATE READ:_____
MY RATING (CIRCLE): ★ ★ ★ ★ ★
MY COMMENTS:_____
_____

☐ Book 7:
I Read It!

SUMMARY:_____
_____
_____

DATE READ:_____
MY RATING (CIRCLE): ★ ★ ★ ★ ★
MY COMMENTS:_____
_____

COLLECTOR'S VALUE GUIDE™

COLLECTING HARRY POTTER

Since the start of the Harry Potter craze, kids and adults alike have been anxiously awaiting the opportunity to purchase products with the likeness of Harry and his friends from Hogwarts. The first printings of each Harry Potter book have already become among the most valuable collectibles around, and surely some of the forthcoming Harry Potter products will also become coveted collectibles.

This "Harry Potter Clock" is one of the licensed Harry Potter products available at Warner Bros. Studio Stores.

To date, over 40 companies have been awarded licenses by Warner Bros. to produce Harry Potter products such as T-shirts, figurines, stuffed animals, clocks, toys and the like. So, no matter what kind of Harry Potter product or collectible you're looking for, chances are that someone's hard at work making your dreams come true.

START YOUR SHOPPING LIST HERE!

"Hermione™ The Bookworm" is a new Secret Box™ by Department 56®

When many people think of collecting, they tend to think of figurines and ornaments. Versions of these products will soon be available throughout the country from several well-known companies. Enesco®, the manufacturer of PRECIOUS MOMENTS® figurines, has a line of Harry Potter merchandise planned, while Department 56® is releasing a line of Harry Potter hinged boxes!

Wizards of the Coast, the company behind the blockbuster Pokémon™ Trading Card Game, is preparing to release a game based on Harry's adventures at Hogwarts. And while they might not fall into the category of traditional collectibles, keep in mind that Mattel has been named the "Master Toy Licensee" and will soon begin production on products that will surely have Harry Potter enthusiasts lined up in stores. And that's just the beginning! Computer games, board games, craft kits and model trains are also among the new toys set to be released in the near future.

Dressing The Part

If you're the type of person who likes to wear your collection rather than store it in a display case, licensed Harry Potter clothing is just the right thing for you. From hats and T-shirts to socks and slippers, you will soon be able to cover yourself from head to toe in Harry Potter attire! Designs are now available in Warner Bros. Studio Stores around the country and will be distributed to major department stores and discount stores in the coming months.

The "Harry Potter Logo Tee," available at Warner Bros. Studio Stores, is one of the many new clothing items that will feature Harry Potter.

Have A Great Feast In The Comfort Of Your Castle

The "Quidditch" beach towel by TerriSol depicts an action-packed scene.

Turn your humble home into a magnificent castle with some of the many home furnishings that are set to be produced. Products expected to be released include children's furniture, decorative throws, bath towels, beach towels, bath accessories and bedding, all of which are the perfect way to add a little magic to your room.

If you're already planning a party, or are just looking for an excuse to have one, the new Harry Potter party products are sure to provide inspiration. From balloons to cake decorations, nearly everything you need to have a fabulous Harry Potter-themed party will soon be available in a store near you.

If you're looking for a gift to bring to the host of a Harry Potter party, picture frames and mugs are currently available in Warner Bros. stores and are expected to arrive at other retailers by the end of 2000. Harry Potter calendars

Enhance your party with party supplies from Hallmark, such as this plate, napkin and cup set.

are perfect for keeping track of appointments, while journals will help any aspiring wizard keep track of their spells.

Harry Potter and his magical merchandising will soon be making his way to a store near you! Some products will make their debut on December 26, 2000, others in Spring 2001 and even more will become available during the back-to-school season in 2001 (just in time for the movie's November release). On the other hand, a few products can be found in stores now. For a look at some of them, check out our spotlight on Warner Bros. Studio Store merchandise beginning on page 63.

"Hedwig the Owl" mug available at the Warner Bros. Studio Store.

While it is impossible to predict exactly which products will become collectible, Harry Potter products are certain to be among the most popular gifts during the holiday season in 2000 and 2001. The exciting part about right now is that this is the first wave of releases, making everything a first edition. So, just as Harry is always on the lookout for that elusive Golden Snitch, be sure to keep your eyes peeled for Harry Potter products! There's no better day than today to start collecting!

You can carry your Harry Potter collection in this backpack from the Warner Bros. Studio Store.

HARRY POTTER IN THE HEADLINES

In just three short years, four books whose names all have started with *"Harry Potter and the . . ."* have put a spell on children around the world. Let's take a look at the stories that have made headlines ever since Harry made his way from Hogwarts to the United States!

LIGHTS! CAMERA! MAGIC!

Harry Potter and the Sorcerer's Stone, the movie, will be casting its spell on theaters in November of 2001. Distributed by Warner Bros., who bought the Harry Potter movie rights in 1998, the film will be full of magic, mystery and fun. Chris Columbus, director of *Home Alone*; *Home Alone 2: Lost in New York*; *Mrs. Doubtfire*; *Nine Months*; *Stepmom* and *Bicentennial Man*, has been announced by Warner Bros. as director of the upcoming film.

J. K. Rowling will keep her creative juices flowing as author of the best-selling book series – bringing the fifth book to the world in 2001 – while also giving valuable advice to the moviemakers. Another important role in the film production is the screenwriter. Steven Kloves has tackled that job as he has adapted the children's best-selling book into a movie script masterpiece that is ready for production.

Filming for this adventurous and "spell-tacular" adaptation of the Harry Potter book series will begin in the fall of 2000, in England, the beloved home of our favorite mystical wizard. Filming will reportedly take place at Leavesden Studios, the former production site of *Star Wars: Episode I – The Phantom Menace*, and also at Britain's 900-year-old Gloucester Cathedral, which will be transformed into the Hogwarts School of Witchcraft and Wizardry. Warner Bros. has a large budget to make Harry's world of magic and fun a silver screen hit! Harry Potter fans should expect the film to be full of special effects and computer-generated images.

Hogwarts School, as depicted on Tri-Star Merchandise's "Houses of Hogwarts Musical Jewelry Box."

Cast In Stone

After months of searching for the perfect young wizard, Warner Bros. announced in August that the character of Harry Potter had been magically discovered and finally cast from a field of thousands of applicants. The young British actor, Daniel Radcliffe, will bring magic to the screen as he plays the mystical Harry Potter. Daniel, who is 11 years old, played the part of young David in the BBC presentation of *David Copperfield*.

The kids have been cast! From left to right in this press release photo: Emma Watson will play Hermione, Daniel Radcliffe will portray Harry Potter and Rupert Grint is Ron Weasley. Photo by Terry O'Neill, courtesy of Warner Bros.

Later in 2000, Daniel can be seen in *The Tailor of Panama*, a John Boorman film.

Eleven-year-old Rupert Grint and 10-year-old Emma Watson, will also bring magic to the screen as they play Ron Weasley and Hermione Granger – Harry's best friends. These two British children are newcomers to the world of stage and screen but have both performed in school drama productions.

ALMOST HARRY!

For David Gale, a 12-year-old boy who lives in the town of Southampton in Hampshire, England, May 22, 2000 will always be remembered as "the most amazing day" of his entire life. You see, that was the day that David auditioned for the role of Harry Potter in the upcoming movie. He was one of the 400 lucky boys who were selected out of a group of over 60,000.

David Gale recalls the day he almost became Harry Potter.

At the end of 1999, word went out that the movie's casting director in London, Susie Figgis, was searching for boys between the ages of 10 and 12, of a specific height and with experience in drama. Following a persistent barrage of letters to Ms. Figgis, David Heyman, the producer, and the Harry Potter Productions offices at Pinewood Studios in Camden Town, London, David was notified that he was one of the 400 chosen to audition!

David travelled by train with his father to the audition location in London where he was joined by what "seemed like thousands of boys," got a picture taken and was asked to sit and wait. David admitted that, at this point, he became "very, very, VERY nervous and got butterflies" in his stomach. He was then taken to another room with a group of twenty other boys. They were told that Steven Spielberg, who was then being considered for the position, may be directing the movie. David told CheckerBee that when he heard this, his "feet almost gave way" and that it was "jolly lucky that they told me that I could sit down" at that moment!

When it was his turn to speak, David suddenly felt completely at ease and told the interviewers about his love of Harry – he has read all of the books at least six times and thinks they are the best books he has read so far – and his love of acting. Before he knew it, the audition was over and David was told that he would get a call within a month if he was chosen for the role. Although he never received that call, David told CheckerBee that he "wouldn't have missed the day for anything and at least I can say on my future [resume], 'I was selected to audition for the first Harry Potter movie.'"

AND IT ALL BEGAN WITH A BOOK . . .

Thousands of children with their parents in tow lined up at the doors of their favorite bookstores, including Barnes & Noble, Waldenbooks, Media Play and B. Dalton, to receive their copies of *Harry Potter and the Goblet of Fire*. Almost like waiting for a concert ticket, fans were there long before the midnight opening on July 8, 2000 to get first crack at the series' fourth book.

And the wait was one big party! Many of the stores engaged the waiting children in Harry Potter trivia competitions and games while employees, who were dressed as wizards and witches, handed out temporary lightning bolt tattoos and black plastic eyeglasses to the crowds. Other stores served coffee to bleary-eyed parents while the younger set (and some older folks too) chose to feast on the jelly beans, candy and jelly-filled doughnuts.

Harry Potter promo pin worn by bookstore employees to promote Book Four.

Although publishers have tried to keep up with the demand by printing over 6 million copies of this latest book in the Harry Potter series, most bookstores found their shelves empty of *Goblet of Fire* within 24 hours. Internet booksellers took advance orders that numbered over 700,000 copies – making *Harry Potter and the Goblet of Fire* a best-seller even before before the book's official release date.

The U.S. cover of *Harry Potter and the Goblet of Fire* by J. K. Rowling.

HOLIDAY DISPLAYS OF HARRY

Potter fans who live in the Chicago and Minneapolis areas will have a visual treat this holiday season. The story of Harry Potter will be transformed into window displays in Chicago's Marshall Fields store on State Street and in Dayton's auditorium display in Minneapolis. Both displays will be open to the public during the store's regular business hours.

Harry Potter In The Headlines

"For more than 35 years, the holiday traditions of Dayton's and Marshall Fields have brought families together," said Rob Gruen, Executive VP for Worldwide Marketing, Warner Bros. Consumer Products, in a press release. He also stated "we are pleased that Harry Potter – which has brought families together the world over to read these magical books – will be celebrated as part of these time-honored events."

Braille Version Hits The Shelves

The Boston-based non-profit braille printing and publishing house, National Braille Press, recently made news when they accomplished the superhuman feat of producing the braille version of *Harry Potter and the Goblet of Fire* in record time. In only 20 days, the 31-person staff of the National Braille Press translated, embossed and collated the first print run of 500 copies – over half-a-million braille pages! The 734-page book translates into 1,184 braille pages and was also published as a floppy disk PortaBook™ which is read on a portable braille reading device.

Louis Braille
(1809-1852)

. . . devised the system of printing and writing for blind people by using one to six raised dots arranged to form recognizable patterns. Representing letters, numbers and punctuation, Braille's patterns are read with the fingertips and is the raised-dot system that has gained universal acceptance.

HARRY BATTLES FOR THE HEARTS OF CHILDREN AND ADULTS

Harry Potter is the number-one selling children's book series, with millions of copies sold worldwide. In fact, each book has hit #1 on the *New York Times* best-seller list. Yet, with the series' seemingly universal appeal, a lot of people have had difficulty classifying the books. Are they for children? Or are they for adults?

Adult cover

Children's cover

The British edition of *Harry Potter and the Prisoner of Azkaban* is available with either an adult or children's cover design.

That confusion helped spark a controversy in January 2000 in the U.K., when Rowling's third book, *Harry Potter and the Prisoner of Azkaban*, finished second to Seamus Heaney's translation of the classic poem *Beowulf* in the race for the prestigious Whitbred Book of the Year prize. At the same award ceremony, Rowling's book walked away with the Children's Book of the Year prize. Some critics felt that *Harry Potter and the Prisoner of Azkaban* should have won both awards, and theorized that the book may have lost because of the perception that Rowling's books belong in the children's literature category – a "label" that millions of adult Harry Potter readers might question.

Kids Vs. Grown-ups, Part Two

Meanwhile, another similar controversy arose in the United States in July 2000. The *New York Times* decided to add a children's best-seller list to its weekly *Book Review* section. As a result of the change, the Harry Potter books, which routinely took up several of the top slots on the regular (and prestigious) best-seller list, were moved to the children's list. Then in September 2000, the *New York Times* divided the children's list into three categories (picture books, paperbacks and chapter books) to appear on a rotating schedule in the *Book Review*. Although some publishers and booksellers have applauded the changes because it increases exposure to children's books, others say the best-selling Harry Potter books are being "squeezed out" by the *New York Times*.

Harry Gets Banned!?!

People who have lamented the decline of reading among today's children have rejoiced at the amazing Harry Potter phenomenon. Educators and parents everywhere are hoping that the series' legions of fans will turn to other exciting books as well. However, not everyone has expressed their love for Harry, usually due to concerns over the themes of witchcraft and magic or over Harry's sometimes mischievous antics.

Over the years, many literary classics have been challenged by censors – including William Golding's *Lord of the Flies*, J.D. Salinger's *The Catcher in the Rye* and Harper Lee's *To Kill a Mockingbird* – and the Harry Potter books haven't been immune to controversy. In November of 1999, for example, the Zeeland, Michigan School District Superintendent of Schools placed restrictions on Harry Potter "read-alouds" in the classroom, removed books from displays in elementary school libraries and required parental permission to check out these books or use them for book reports.

At a May 11, 2000 press conference, however, the superintendent rescinded many of the restrictions that he imposed in November. Children in the Zeeland School District are now able to find Harry Potter on their school library's bookshelves and can check out the titles without written permission from their parents. Hip, hip, hooray!

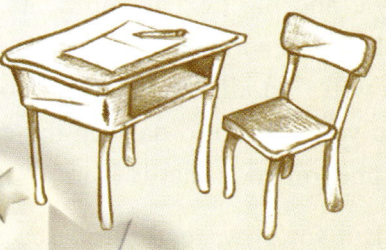

Harry's Heroes

In September 2000, a group of citizens were honored for their efforts in opposing Harry Potter bans in their communities by the American Library Association at a ceremony held at the Library of Congress in Washington, D.C. Two of the honorees were from Zeeland, Michigan (see previous story), who organized a group to counteract restrictions on the Harry Potter books in their school district. Teenagers from California and New Jersey were also honored for bringing the story of Harry

Potter to groups of low-income children through "read-alouds" and by organizing a letter-writing campaign to combat an effort to remove the Potter books from libraries. When the Dursleys locked up Harry's books during the summer, he probably wished he had these heroes in his corner!

Tomorrow's Headlines

As the shopping season kicks into gear for the upcoming holidays, be prepared to see and hear even more about Harry! Watch for the latest product information in store advertisements, on television and on the Internet, especially on CheckerBee's web site, located at *www.CollectorsQuest.com*. There, you will also find the latest scoop on the upcoming movie and the next installments in the Harry Potter series of books. At *www.CollectorsQuest.com*, you will find all you need to know to keep yourself up-to-date on the exciting phenomenon that is Harry Potter!

But for now, read on to see what else Harry Potter fans are up to.

Harry Potter Enchants The World Wide Web

The Harry Potter phenomenon has undoubtedly made its mark on the world of literature. This series of books has inspired a reading frenzy, with all four books becoming bestsellers. Reports abound of children claiming that although they never read, they just can't put down the Harry Potter books. In fact, it was even reported that many children were seen reading the beginning chapters of *Harry Potter and the Goblet of Fire* as they left the cash registers after camping out for the book on the night of its debut.

Enesco's mini figurine of Hermione, one of the characters made popular in the books.

And his popularity reaches far beyond bookshelves. Harry Potter has also spawned a majestic world with a constantly growing Internet community. For official Harry Potter news, including updates on the upcoming film, you will want to click on *harrypotter.com*, the official Warner Bros. Harry Potter web site.

You can also stay informed by regularly visiting CheckerBee's web site, *www.CollectorsQuest.com*, for up-to-date Harrry Potter news and information, including bulletin boards and new product releases.

A Click Of A Mouse And Off You Go!

You can find tons of fan sites all over the web. But where should you look? Type "Harry Potter" or "J. K. Rowling" into a search engine and see what you find. There will likely be a huge listing, so have fun picking your adventures! If you're looking for something more specific, add other terms such as "games" or "collectibles" to your search. The Internet has become a place where fans can express their creativity and find the latest news about Harry and his creator, J. K. Rowling, especially in the areas of fan fiction, role-playing games and rumors.

Fan Fiction Stirs The Imagination

Loyal readers of Harry Potter have found a creative outlet for their wizardry fantasies. The Internet abounds with fan-created sites which showcase a wide variety of activities.

A vast majority of the Harry Potter web sites developed by fans include a section entitled "fan fiction." By clicking onto a fan fiction site, fans enter their own world of Harry Potter; a world full of magic, fantasy and enchantment. Fan fiction sites include a wide variety of activities. The most popular type of fan fiction is the creation of your own story featuring Harry Potter and his life of broomsticks, wands and magical powers. Another fan fiction

option is to develop a new character and place that new wizard or non-magical character within the Harry Potter story line.

ROLE-PLAYING WITH HARRY POTTER

Another very popular activity is role-playing games, where average people can enter a land of make-believe. In this type of game, the player takes on the persona of either an existing Harry Potter character or one that the player makes up. Then, as the character, the person enters into conversation with other players and lives out a story line. When playing these games you can become a student at Hogwarts, visit Diagon Alley, take wizard classes, play Quidditch or relax in your house common room.

"Hedwig the Owl" stuffed animal available at the Warner Bros. Studio Stores.

Other activities include writing a "howler" (delivered by owls in the Harry Potter books) to send to your favorite Hogwarts student or teacher, making or taking Harry Potter quizzes, solving crossword puzzles or word searches and much more!

MAGICAL SPECULATIONS & RUMORS

Most Harry Potter fans remain fascinated with Harry's life of magic even when they are not currently reading about the young wizard. And as some fans still can't get enough of this universe, a popular way for fans to stay up to date with Harry Potter's world of mystery, magic, and fun is to speculate and gossip about the new adventures that will unfold in the next three story lines.

Most of these rumors are generated by fans as they read for clues and hints given during J. K. Rowling's interviews or in magazine articles. Sometimes information comes from someone who claims to have an inside connection. At times, these rumors are right on the money, but other times they are way off.

So what do you think? Will "You-Know-Who" ever show his face again? Will there ever be a love interest in Harry's life? What will become of Hagrid's fascination with strange and magical pets? How will Mr. Weasley balance his job at the Ministry of Magic and his fondness for creating forbidden items such as the Ford Anglia? What will be the fate of the next Defense Against the Dark Arts teacher? Will we continue to learn more about Harry's real family?

It can be quite interesting to keep an eye out for these rumors and then to compare them to what actually does happen in the story when the next three books are actually released.

Fans can also enter a wide range of Harry Potter chat rooms and clubs to discuss what they love most about the wizard and his adventures at Hogwarts. Some clubs specialize and focus in on one aspect of the Harry Potter phenomenon.

THE KIDS GO HIGH-TECH

One of the more exciting results of Harry Potter's popularity is the involvement of children in the process of web page production. As you browse any number of sites about Harry on the Internet, you may be surprised to discover that a large majority of them are created and maintained by fans under the age of 18.

HARRY, HARRY EVERYWHERE

With all the Harry Potter merchandise beginning to hit stores and the wide range of topics available on the Internet, every aspect of the Harry Potter phenomenon can be bought, found and talked about with fans all over the world. If Harry somehow knew how many people were out there in cyberspace ready to support him in times of need, he might not be so fearful of "You-Know-Who." In just a few short years, the books have an inspired a massive and interactive community on the Internet. Enjoy your quest for more Harry Potter fun, right on your home computer!

"You-Know-Who" as portrayed on a T-Shirt from Warner Bros. Studio Stores.

Around The Globe With Harry Potter

The Harry Potter books have now been published in over 30 languages and are available in over 100 countries, with more on the way. Let's hop onto our brooms and take a spin around the globe to see some different versions of Harry Potter! For a look at the international book covers, please see the "International Books" section beginning on page 111.

North America

English-speaking children who live in **Canada** read a version of the Harry Potter books printed by Raincoast Books. *Harry Potter and the Sorcerer's Stone*, the first book of the series, was published in the **United States** by Scholastic Press in 1998. Some British terminology that was used in the original English version was "Americanized" to make it easier for children to understand. Artist Mary GrandPré provided illustrations.

South America

To the south of the United States, Castilian Spanish is spoken in many countries of **Latin America**. With cover designs by Dolores Avendaño, the Castilian versions of Harry Potter are currently printed in Argentina and Barcelona, Spain. Translated into Portuguese by Lia Wyler, the

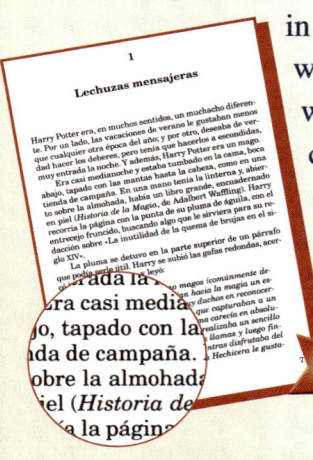

The first page of Chapter One in the Castilian Spanish version of Book 3.

Harry Potter books printed in Rio de Janeiro for readers in **Brazil** feature cover art by Mary GrandPré and a single interior design of the Hogwarts Crest on the title page.

AFRICA

Flying east over the Atlantic Ocean, we reach Africa. According to Human & Rousseau Ltd. in **South Africa**, the company printing Harry Potter for readers in this southernmost African country, an Afrikaans translation of Harry Potter is now available.

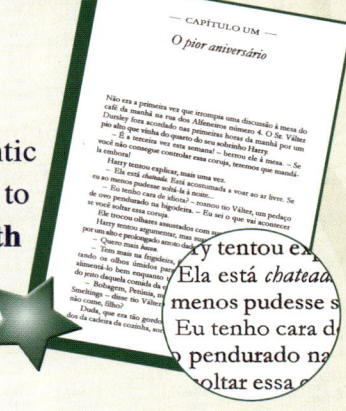

The first page of Chapter One in the Portuguese (Brazil) version of Book 2.

EUROPE

Let's fly north to where it all began! In 1997, the first book of the series was published in **Great Britain** by Bloomsbury Publishing. Bloomsbury also printed books with featured cover art done by a variety of artists and others with "adult" covers for older fans of the series! For Harry Potter fans in **Portugal**, the books have been translated into Portuguese by Isabel Fraga and feature cover art by Mary GrandPré. In **France,** the covers of the translations are illustrated by Jean-Claude Götting and feature scenes of Harry, Hermione and Ron dressed in pointy black hats and robes.

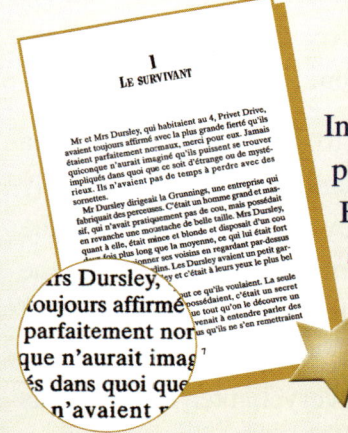

The first page of Chapter One in the French version of Book 1.

Since J. K. Rowling studied French, she could have translated this one herself!

With cover designs by Alvaro Tapia and chapters separated by dark pages filled with stars, translations from **Sweden** feature a sprinkling of starry designs. Stars are also featured in the translations in **Norway**, where a large starburst is found at the beginning of each chapter. For readers in **The Netherlands**, Dutch versions feature cover art by Ien van Laanen. A publishing firm in Helsinki, **Finland** has printed Finnish Harry Potter books with colorful cover designs featuring a curly-haired Harry, freckled Ron and buck-toothed Hermione!

The first page of Chapter One in the Swedish version of Book 1.

Thanks to illustrator Serena Rigietti, readers in **Italy** can actually see Dudley with a pig's tail and the troll terrorizing Hermione in the girl's bathroom! Line drawings of an owl appear at the top of the first page of everychapter in the books translated into Hungarian.

The first page of Chapter One in the Italian version of Book 1.

Denmark and **Iceland** have also published translations for their countries as well as **Germany, Greece,** the **Czech Republic, Croatia, Bulgaria, Romania, Poland, Estonia, Slovenia** and a Catalan version for readers in **Spain.**

ASIA

Travelling east toward Asia, you will discover that the covers of the books printed in **China** and **Japan** and also in **Israel** are printed on what Americans consider to be the back of the book and that the story begins in the back. This is because these languages are read from right to left.

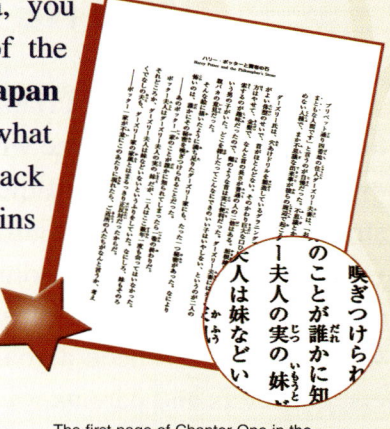

The first page of Chapter One in the Japanese version of Book 1.

Because of the space necessary for the characters used in the Korean language, each Harry Potter title translated in **Korea** is split into two separate books. In **Indonesia**, the Harry Potter books are translated into the language of Bahasa Indonesian. Translations for readers in the countries of **Thailand** and **Turkey** will be published soon.

The first page of Chapter One in the Korean version of Book 1.

...WITH MORE TO COME!

Our brooms have gotten quite a workout on our whirlwind journey around the world! We can expect many more countries to publish translations of the Harry Potter books – a world wide phenomenon!

Harry Potter In The Schools

With the character of Harry Potter, J. K. Rowling has introduced children to someone with whom they can relate. Almost everyone has experienced the battles with the class bully, the stress over exams and the thrill of playing their favorite sport. Consequently, kids are reading the Harry Potter series for the pure enjoyment of it, a pleasant trend which has always been a goal of teachers, educators and parents.

In classrooms around the country, teachers are beginning to incorporate this wildly popular series of books into their lesson plans in a variety of subjects by engaging their students in classroom activities and discussions. In addition to the variety of resources that can be found on the Internet, three literature guides for teachers have been published by Scholastic Inc., a leading source for classroom materials.

As upcoming installments of Harry's life are published, teachers and parents will be able to locate additional materials on how to encourage good reading habits and capitalize on a renewed interest in literature led by Harry Potter.

Available in teacher supply stores, bookstores and on the Scholastic web site, these teacher's guides provide activities and questions appropriate for children in grades 4 through 8.

Harry Potter and the Sorcerer's Stone Literature Guide

Scholastic's guide to the first book in the series, *Harry Potter and the Sorcerer's Stone*, leads teachers and children through the intricacies of the novel, including a character guide, a summary of the basic plot and some of the major themes that play a role.

In addition to the summaries and discussion prompts for each chapter of the book, Scholastic has included a timeline poster, a biography of the author and ideas for group and class projects.

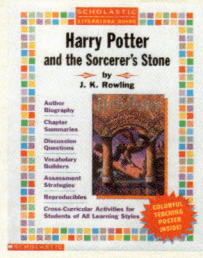

The cover of Scholastic's teacher's guide to the first Harry Potter book.

Also, there are cross-curricular activities including a writing a script for a radio broadcast of a Quidditch match play-by-play and drawing floor plans of the Hogwarts School, based on descriptions of the castle's classrooms from the book.

Harry Potter and the Chamber of Secrets Literature Guide

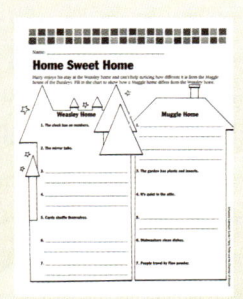

A sample inside page of the second teacher's guide.

In Scholastic's guide for teaching the second book in the series, *Harry Potter and the Chamber of Secrets*, educators will find suggestions for a social studies lesson involving a study of the geography of London and a writing lesson on composing cheers to perform at an imaginary Quidditch match. An art activity which charts the colors that are described in the book and a science lesson on spider research are also included. A poster on the "cause and effect" of story elements is inside this guide.

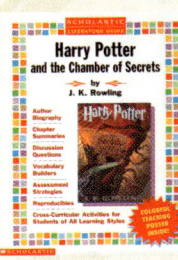

HARRY POTTER AND THE PRISONER OF AZKABAN LITERATURE GUIDE

The poster in Scholastic's guide for teaching the third book, *Harry Potter and the Prisoner of Azkaban*, invites students to "peer into the crystal globe" and identify objects that play an important role in Harry's third year at Hogwarts.

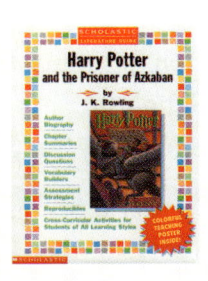

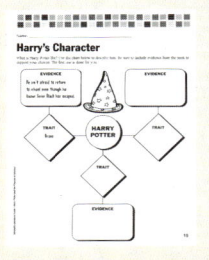

Another suggestion includes creating a Hogwarts school newspaper where the students fill the roles of reporter, editor, proofreader and others. Science lessons on astronomy and writing lessons involving fortune telling can also add spice to the classroom.

OTHER TEACHING AIDES AND GUIDES

As teachers and educators prepare lessons and evaluate their effectiveness in classrooms, more activities will be added to those already on Internet web sites devoted to Harry Potter. Other teaching materials are expected to be published soon, so keep an eye out for new and exciting ways to encourage reading and stimulate your child's imagination!

J. K. Rowling: A Wizard Of Words

Best-selling author J. K. Rowling.

Like Harry Potter, who grew up not realizing his incredible potential, J. K. Rowling probably never imagined the immense success that her Harry Potter books would bring. Since the publication of her first book, *Harry Potter and the Philosopher's Stone*, (released as *Harry Potter and the Sorcerer's Stone* in the U.S.), her fan base has grown steadily to encompass children and adults all over the world. She has won numerous awards and her books not only make the top of the best-seller lists, but remain there for months at a time!

The Early Years

Joanne Kathleen Rowling was born on July 31, 1965 in Chipping Sodbury General Hospital. A born storyteller, she began making up her own stories at an early age. In fact, less than two years after she was born, Rowling found a captive audience for her tales. Her new sister, Di, proved to be a great listener, especially when the stories involved their favorite subject – rabbits. Rowling's first written story was called *Rabbit* and was about a rabbit – named Rabbit of course – who contracted the measles and was visited by a large bee named Miss Bee.

School soon began for Rowling and it gave her plenty of opportunity to read. Her family moved from the town of Yate (a small town close to the city Bristol) to Winterbourne on the opposite side of Bristol. Two of her best friends in Winterbourne were a brother and sister with the last name of Potter. Ian Potter was very mischievous and enjoyed playing tricks on the girls. The three of them would also dress up as witches and wizards and Rowling would often tell them stories. When Rowling turned 9, her family moved again to the small village of Tutshill. Around this time, she began to read the works of Ian Fleming and eventually those of Jane Austen who is still, to this day, her favorite author. It was also at this time that she began to encounter a great deal of difficulty at school.

Rowling's new school, Tutshill Primary, was small and old-fashioned

King's Cross, London

The King's Cross Railway Station plays an important role, not just in thee Harry Potter books, but also in J. K. Rowling's real life!

• Rowling's parents first met on a train leaving from that station.

• The idea for the series came to Rowling on a train returning to King's Cross.

• The Hogwarts Express leaves from King's Cross' platform 9 3/4.

and her teacher, Mrs. Morgan, was very strict. On Rowling's first day of school, Mrs. Morgan gave her a math test. As Rowling had not yet learned fractions, she failed the test, earning her a seat in the far right of the classroom. Unfortunately, Rowling later found out that this was where Mrs. Morgan sat the kids who she felt weren't very smart. Eventually, however, she managed to improve her teacher's impression of her and managed to move to the left side of the room by the end of the school year.

For Rowling, school seemed to get better and better. She then moved on to Wyedean Comprehensive where she would spend lunch time enthralling her small group of friends with stories. She continued to write, read and tell stories throughout her years at Wyedean and eventually graduated as Head Girl. In fact, the quiet, bookish girl she once was became the inspiration for one of Rowling's characters – Hermione Granger.

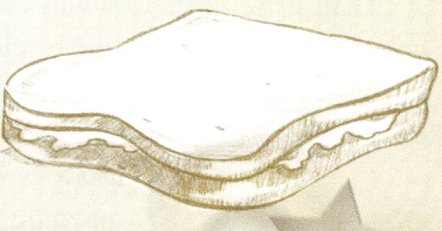

Following her parents' advice after graduation, Rowling enrolled at Exeter University where she studied French and even travelled abroad to Paris for a year. After graduation, she tried her hand at many jobs: she worked for Amnesty International for two years, researching human rights violations in Africa, and she also had a series of secretarial jobs, where instead of paying attention in meetings, Rowling often found herself jotting down story ideas.

One of these secretarial jobs was based in Manchester and she enjoyed the quiet time during the train commute from her home in London to Manchester. It was while gazing out the window on one of these trips in 1990 that she had a flash of inspiration. Why not write a story about a young boy attending wizard school? Thus, Harry Potter was born. Although she didn't have a pen and paper with her, Rowling continued to develop the concept and, after arriving home, she began to write story lines for the novel.

TRYING TIMES

That same year, Rowling's 45-year-old mother, who had been diagnosed with multiple sclerosis, died. Shortly after her mother's death, the author accepted a job in Portugal teaching English as a foreign language. While in Portugal, she continued to write about Harry. Meanwhile, a romantic story line was unfolding in the author's personal life. She fell in love with, and married, a Portuguese television journalist. Unfortunately, their marriage wasn't destined to last and, shortly after the birth of their daughter Jessica in 1993, the couple divorced. Rowling moved to Edinburgh, Scotland on the advice of her sister, Di, who now lived there. She bundled up her daughter, her possessions and several chapters of her Harry Potter story and began the next chapter of her own life.

Being a single mother was difficult, and Rowling often

> **What's In A Name**
>
> Harry Potter author J. K. Rowling named her daughter after human rights activist Jessica Mitford, a woman she greatly admires.

found herself short of funds. She did not qualify for state-sponsored child care and, even with public assistance, she could not afford to pay for Jessica's day care. She knew that if she concentrated on her writing she could finish Harry's story, so she chose to focus on the novel rather than look for another teaching job. Rowling's confidence in her writing had grown by this point, mostly due to the fact that her sister, Di, enjoyed the concept. She began taking Jessica to cafés, where, with a small purchase, she could sit quietly for hours and write. These were very productive times and, in 1995, the first Harry Potter story was finished.

Success At Last!

Now Rowling had to find an agent and a publisher. She didn't have the money to make photocopies of her manuscript, so she typed up copies on her old, second-hand typewriter. She sent out the novel to a few agents and publishers that seemed to be the best prospects and kept her fingers crossed. Meanwhile, she applied for, and received, a rather sizeable grant from the Scottish Arts Council, which would enable her to complete a second Harry Potter book. She accepted a job as a French teacher in Edinburgh and thought up a story line for the second Harry Potter book.

While concentrating on the second Harry Potter novel, Rowling anxiously awaited word on the fate of the first. Finally, an envelope arrived in the mail from one of the agents. Inside, a letter said that agent Christopher Little would be glad to represent her! After several rejections from publishers, Little introduced Rowling to Bloomsbury Publishing, an independent publisher, who bought the book in 1996. Rowling only received a modest sum from the company, but she was thrilled. In June 1997, *Harry Potter and the Philosopher's Stone* was published in England. It was an immediate success.

> **Initial Fears**
>
> J. K. Rowling's publisher was worried that young boys would not read a book written by a woman so they asked the author to use her initials.

Word of mouth spread and when the time came for international publishers to bid on the book, Arthur Levine from Scholastic Books paid an unheard of advance for a first-time children's author. In 1998, the book was released in the U.S. as *Harry Potter and the Sorcerer's Stone* and was just as successful as its overseas counterpart.

By this point, Rowling had already written the second book, *Harry Potter and the Chamber of Secrets*, which was released in England in July 1998. One year later, the third novel in the series, *Harry Potter and the Prisoner of Azkaban*, was released and immediately jumped to #1 on the best-seller lists.

Rowling then began her fourth book which had a working title of *Harry Potter and the Doomspell Tournament*. On July 8, 2000, the fourth edition of the series was released simultaneously in England and the U.S with the title *Harry Potter and the Goblet of Fire*. It had an initial print run of 5.3 million copies – 1.5 million in Britain and 3.8 million in the U.S. Fans everywhere lined up for special midnight sales of the book.

> ### Room For One More
> J. K. Rowling is scheduled to participate in the October 2000 International Festival of Authors where she will hold a reading in Toronto's 55,000-seat SkyDome – the only place large enough to hold all of her fans!

Harry Potter has entranced fans all over the globe. The books have been published in over 100 countries and in more than 30 different languages. The first three books alone have sold over 30 million copies, while film rights for the first two books were purchased by Warner Bros. And Rowling herself has not been unaffected by her sudden fame. She won an "Author of the Year" award from the Booksellers Association in both 1999 and 2000 and a "Children's Book of the Year" award at the 2000 British Book Awards. Rowling has been appointed as an OBE (Officer of the British Empire) and has received honorary doctorate degrees from both her alma mater, Exeter University, and the University of St. Andrews in Scotland. She is now one of the highest paid women in Britain and recently ranked 24th in earnings in *Forbes* magazine's "Celebrity 100." Rowling's book

This is the cover of the Dutch edition of the first Harry Potter book.

signings are consistently mobbed by fans and reporters clamor for interviews.

The enormous popularity of Harry Potter has even affected her British publisher. Bloomsbury editor Emma Matthewson had to guard the manuscript for the fourth book very closely. When not working on it, she kept it in a bank vault and she never brought it to the publisher's offices. In apparent attempts to steal the manuscript, she was mugged once and her car was broken into twice. In June 2000, two reporters broke into the British printers and had to be led out by security. Perhaps the biggest proof of the public's insatiable appetite for Harry is the fact that the fifth book is already topping the advance order charts at *Amazon.com* before it has even been written!

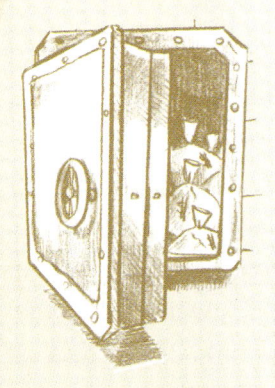

Perhaps part of her success is due to the fact that Rowling didn't consider her audience when writing the first Harry Potter book. She didn't write it to please children or adults – she just wrote what she liked. Writing the Harry Potter novels got her through some tough times in her life and the characters have all become near and dear to her. It is truly a labor of love.

A Portrait Of The Artists

Fantastic illustrations, along with J. K. Rowling's wonderfully descriptive words, have helped shape our visual image of the characters in each of the Harry Potter books. Here's a look at some of the artists who have illustrated the books worldwide:

United States: Mary GrandPré

Born in South Dakota and raised in Minnesota, Mary GrandPré started her career as a young child when she drew her first picture – a portrait of Mickey Mouse.

She continued to enjoy art throughout her school years, and may have found inspiration not only in the movies but in tales spun by her father, an avid storyteller. She enrolled and studied Fine Art at the Minneapolis College of Art and Design. During this time, GrandPré began to develop her own unique style which she calls "soft geometry" which features a blend of light and pastels.

Mary GrandPré's illustration of Dobby the house-elf from *Harry Potter and the Chamber of Secrets*.

After graduation, GrandPré accepted a number of freelance jobs creating commercial art for ad agencies and corporate clients. In addition to her work with these companies, she sent her portfolio to several publishers and was eventually contacted by the art director at The Crown Publishing

Group, a division of Random House. She was contracted to provide illustrations for a children's book – *Chin Yu Min and the Ginger Cat*, written by Jennifer Armstrong.

The book was published in 1993 and since then, GrandPré has enjoyed much success as a children's book illustrator, providing the art for numerous authors. When Scholastic Books first contacted her to provide artwork for *Harry Potter and the Sorcerer's Stone*, GrandPré didn't think it would be any different than her other assignments. Was she in for a surprise!

Illustration by Mary GrandPré's from *Chin Yu Min and the Ginger Cat*.

To create the art for the first *Harry Potter* book, GrandPré would have to rely on readings of the text and approval from Scholastic. Once she had the publisher's input, she worked on the final art. The cover was done in pastels, while the interior chapter illustrations were done with charcoal. GrandPré will eventually be illustrating all seven books in the series.

GrandPré continues to do commercial illustration and book covers and has future plans to write and illustrate her own children's books. Her art has appeared on magazine covers including *Atlantic Monthly* and *Business Week*. She even did a Harry Potter cover for the September 1999 issue of *Time* magazine. She has also done work for several brochures and pamphlets, including one for the Colorado

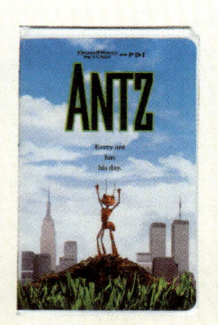

Look for the artistic touches of Mary GrandPré in the 1998 film *Antz*.

Symphony. In 1997, GrandPré's work became a permanent part of the exhibition "Woman Illustrators, Past and Present" run by the Society for Illustrators. GrandPré helped to design several landscapes for the animated film, *Antz,* and was named *Entertainment Weekly*'s "It Imagineer" in 2000. She currently lives in St. Paul, Minnesota and works in a studio attached to her home.

FRANCE: JEAN-CLAUDE GÖTTING

According to his official web site, after studying at the Dupérré School of Arts, Jean-Claude Götting went on to create comic book illustrations for Futuropolis Publishing and for the underground magazine *PLG*. He now focuses his energy on book illustrations and painting. In addition to the Harry Potter novels, Götting has done illustrations for several other books and magazines and his artwork has been featured in galleries around the world.

Jean-Claude Götting illustrated the French cover of the first Harry Potter book.

GREAT BRITAIN: THOMAS TAYLOR, CLIFF WRIGHT & GILES GREENFIELD

Unlike the seven American books which will have the same illustrator, the British editions of the Harry Potter novels have already featured three different artists.

Thomas Taylor was fresh out of art school when he was chosen to create the cover of

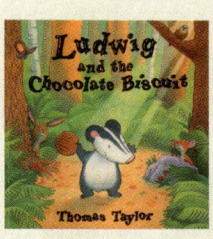

The cover of Thomas Taylor's tale of Ludwig the badger.

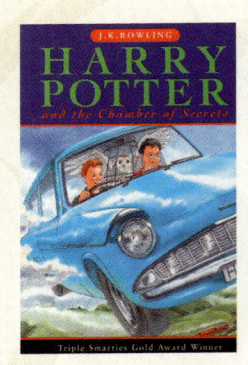

A Portrait Of The Artists

J. K. Rowling's novel of a budding wizard. Taylor has gone on to write and illustrate two children's books.

A writer and illustrator of over 15 children's books, Cliff Wright illustrated both the second and third novels in the Harry Potter series.

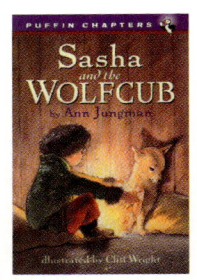

Cliff Wright's illustration of the UK cover of *Harry Potter and the Chamber of Secrets.*

Giles Greenfield illustrated a number of other children's books before being contacted by Bloomsbury to work on the cover art for the fourth Harry Potter novel. His cover design features Harry on his broomstick.

Illustrated by Cliff Wright, the children's book shown here is written by Ann Jungman.

Pictures Of Potter

The following are some of the other illustrators who have provided artwork for Harry Potter books around the globe:

Holland – Ien van Laanen
Spain – Delores Avendaño
Italy – Serena Riglietti
Sweden – Alvaro Tapia
Germany – Sabine Wilharm

Harry Potter Product Showcase

In this section, we will preview many of the exciting Harry Potter products that will be arriving in stores in 2000 and 2001. As you will see, we will often mention some of the magical connections between upcoming products and the amazing events and characters found in the Harry Potter book series. The fantasy world created by J. K. Rowling has certainly inspired the imaginations of the world's leading manufacturers.

The First Years

Warner Bros. Consumer Products, working closely with author J. K. Rowling, is in charge of the Harry Potter licensing program. Because the whole world seems to *love* Harry Potter – boys and girls, kids and adults – Warner Bros. is being very careful to ensure that only the most creative products of the highest quality are introduced into the marketplace, so as not to disappoint the loyal fans of the popular series.

So far, Warner Bros. has granted rights to over 50 companies to produce merchandise based on the first two Harry Potter books. To date, the first products have made their debut at Warner Bros. Studio Stores and more products are being released all the time. A second wave of licensed products will become available only in select retail outlets for the holiday

2000 season. After December 26, 2000, however, more products will be available at other select outlets. A true "mass market" release of products is scheduled for about two months before the release of the first Harry Potter movie which is scheduled to premiere in November 2001.

The early stages of the Harry Potter licensing program mirror Hogwarts society in some ways. The young Hogwarts students aren't allowed to practice magic during the summers – they are encouraged to wait and perform the spells only when they are truly "ready." It takes discipline from both the adult wizards and their children – the wizards and witches "in training" – to adhere to this policy. It's certainly frustrating for Harry Potter and his friends to hold their magic in check, but they know that once they've learned enough, their magical abilities will be powerful and pure.

Warner Bros. is using the same "patience is a virtue" strategy with its carefully planned roll-out of products, which means that, for now, it may be a challenge to find all of your favorite Harry Potter merchandise in stores. But, by the time the movie rolls around – watch out! – the results should come in the form of some wonderful Harry Potter merchandise.

Chapter One – The Bookstores

Bookstores were the first retail outlets to experience the Harry Potter phenomena first-hand, well before the licensing program began. **Scholastic** is the United States publisher for the Harry Potter series and the first four books (of a planned seven) have all been released in hardcover editions. As of October 2000, only *Harry Potter and the Sorcerer's Stone* and *Harry Potter and the Chamber of Secrets* had been released in paperback. The wonderful tales can also be found in other formats, including audio compact discs or cassettes, braille and large print editions. Check your local bookstore to see what they have in stock. Bookstores will also be a great place to look for additional Harry Potter products during the 2000 holiday season and beyond.

Chapter Two – Warner Bros. Studio Stores

In late summer 2000, the first licensed Harry Potter products started shipping exclusively in **Warner Bros. Studio Stores**. There are currently 136 Warner Bros. Studio Stores in 34 states, plus the District of Columbia (for a complete list of stores, see *www.wbstore.com*). If you don't live in a large state like California, Florida, New York or Texas, there may only be one (or none) of these stores in your state, so it may be a challenge to get the early Harry Potter products. Another option you have is to order products directly from the Warner Bros. Studio Store web site.

Among the first products to arrive in Warner Bros. Studio Stores were T-shirts, backpacks, mugs and other back-to-school items. These products are specially labeled for Warner Bros. stores, although most are produced by the licensed manufacturers who will be releasing products to the general market at a later date.

Carry your gear in a "Black Gadgets Backpack" from the Warner Bros. store.

Following, you will find a spotlight on the products that have been available at the Warner Bros. Studio Stores. Be sure to check your local store or the Warner Bros. web site frequently so you don't miss any of the new and exciting Harry Potter merchandise that will appear there – almost as if by magic! After the *Warner Bros. Product Spotlight*, we'll take a look at the many manufacturers who will soon be enchanting the world with licensed Harry Potter merchandise.

Warner Bros. Product Spotlight

Warner Bros. Product Spotlight

Since August 2000, Warner Bros. Studio Stores have been stocked with Harry Potter merchandise including apparel, school supplies, home decor and party goods. Remember, there are new products arriving all the time!

Apparel

For Harry Potter fans who love to wear their collection, this is the place to be! Warner Bros. has had almost 30 styles of T-shirts and sweatshirts available, in addition to hats, bags, watches and a keyring. Let's take a look!

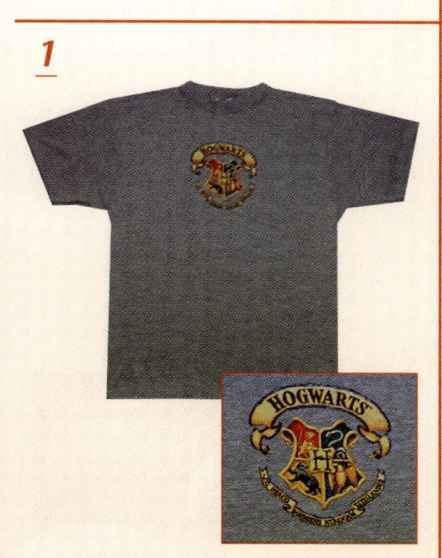

1

Ash Hogwarts Crest Tee (kids' sizes only)
T-shirt • Retail: $12
Item #: BM262 • Issued: 2000

2

Ash Hogwarts Long Sleeve Tee (boys' sizes only)
T-shirt • Retail: $24
Item #: HM152 • Issued: 2000

Harry Potter Product Showcase

Warner Bros. Product Spotlight

Harry Potter Product Showcase

3
Ash Quidditch Tee
(boys' sizes only)
T-shirt • Retail: $16
Item #: HM197 • Issued: 2000

4
Ash Slytherin House Tee
(boys' sizes only)
T-shirt • Retail: $12
Item #: HM198 • Issued: 2000

5
Black Fluffy Tee
(boys' sizes only)
T-shirt • Retail: $12
Item #: HM199 • Issued: 2000

6
Black Name Tee
(boys' sizes only)
T-shirt • Retail: $12
Item #: HM998 • Issued: 2000

COLLECTOR'S VALUE GUIDE™

Warner Bros. Product Spotlight

7

**Black Voldemort Tee
(adult sizes only)**
T-shirt • Retail: $16
Item #: HM200 • Issued: 2000

8

**Black Voldemort Tee
(boys' sizes only)**
T-shirt • Retail: $16
Item #: HM196 • Issued: 2000

9

**Blue Glitter Stars Tee
(girls' sizes only)**
T-shirt • Retail: $14
Item #: GM447 • Issued: 2000

10

**Gryffindor House Tee
(adult sizes only)**
T-shirt • Retail: $16
Item #: CM361 • Issued: 2000

Harry Potter Product Showcase

Warner Bros. Product Spotlight

Harry Potter Product Showcase

11
**Gryffindor House Tee
(kids' sizes only)**
T-shirt • Retail: $12
Item #: CM358 • Issued: 2000

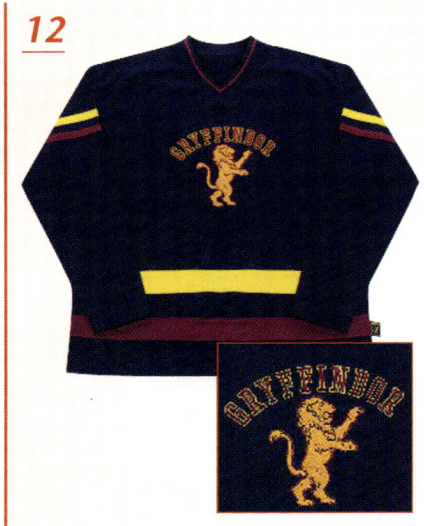

12
**Gryffindor Jersey
(adult sizes only)**
Jersey • Retail: $38
Item #: GM445 • Issued: 2000

13
**Harry Potter Logo Tee
(kids' sizes only)**
T-shirt • Retail: $12
Item #: CM299 • Issued: 2000

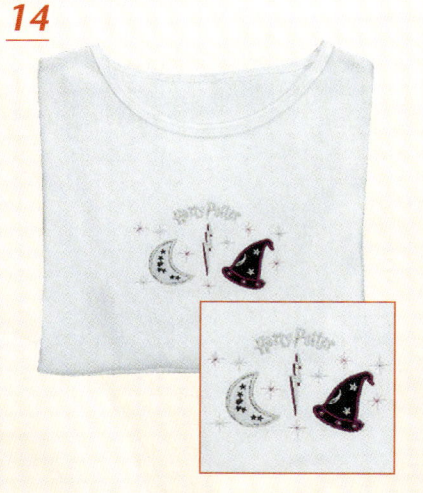

14
**Harry Potter Long
Sleeve Tee
(girls' sizes only)**
T-shirt • Retail: $14
Item #: GM446 • Issued: 2000

COLLECTOR'S VALUE GUIDE™

Warner Bros. Product Spotlight

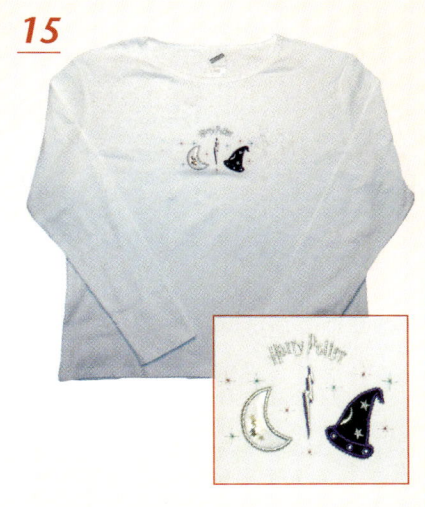

15
Harry Potter Long Sleeve Tee
(ladies' sizes only)
T-shirt • Retail: $24
Item #: HM231 • Issued: 2000

16
Hufflepuff House Tee
(kids' sizes only)
T-shirt • Retail: $12
Item #: DM503 • Issued: 2000

17
Navy Hogwarts Crest Tee
(adult sizes only)
T-shirt • Retail: $16
Item #: BM263 • Issued: 2000

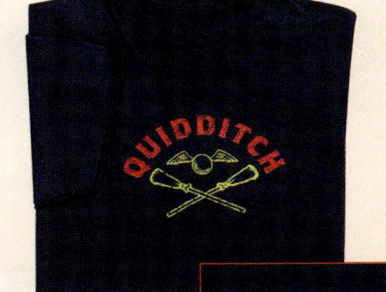

18
Navy Quidditch Tee
(adult sizes only)
T-shirt • Retail: $16
Item #: HM245 • Issued: 2000

Harry Potter Product Showcase

COLLECTOR'S VALUE GUIDE™

Warner Bros. Product Spotlight

Harry Potter Product Showcase

19

**Pink Cauldron Pocket Tee
(girls' sizes only)**
T-shirt • Retail: $12
Item #: GM371 • Issued: 2000

20

**Pink Glitter Stars Tee
(girls' sizes only)**
T-shirt • Retail: $14
Item #: GM448 • Issued: 2000

21

**Pink Tilted Pocket Tee
(girls' sizes only)**
T-shirt • Retail: $12
Item #: GM372 • Issued: 2000

22

**Plum Long Sleeve Tee
(ladies' sizes only)**
T-shirt • Retail: $24
Item #: HM232 • Issued: 2000

COLLECTOR'S
VALUE GUIDE™

Warner Bros. Product Spotlight

Harry Potter Product Showcase

23
**Purple Hogwarts Crest Tee
(girls' sizes only)**
T-shirt • Retail: $12
Item #: HM999 • Issued: 2000

24
**Ravenclaw House Tee
(kids' sizes only)**
T-shirt • Retail: $12
Item #: CM360 • Issued: 2000

25
**Slytherin House Tee
(adult sizes only)**
T-shirt • Retail: $16
Item #: LD003 • Issued: 2000

26
**Slytherin House Tee
(kids' sizes only)**
T-shirt • Retail: $12
Item #: CM359 • Issued: 2000

COLLECTOR'S
VALUE GUIDE™

Warner Bros. Product Spotlight

Harry Potter Product Showcase

27
**Turquoise Sorting Hat Tee
(kids' sizes only)**
T-shirt • Retail: $12
Item #: HM194 • Issued: 2000

28
**Black Winter Fleece
Pullover
(adult sizes only)**
Sweatshirt • Retail: $38
Item #: HM204 • Issued: 2000

29
**Charcoal Hogwarts Fleece
(boys' sizes only)**
Sweatshirt • Retail: $26
Item #: HM154 • Issued: 2000

30
Black Gadgets Backpack
Bag • Retail: $22
Item #: GM367 • Issued: 2000

COLLECTOR'S VALUE GUIDE™

Warner Bros. Product Spotlight

31
Gray Gryffindor Backpack
Bag • Retail: $22
Item #: HM169 • Issued: 2000

32
Pink Quilted Backpack
Bag • Retail: $12
Item #: N/A • Issued: 2000

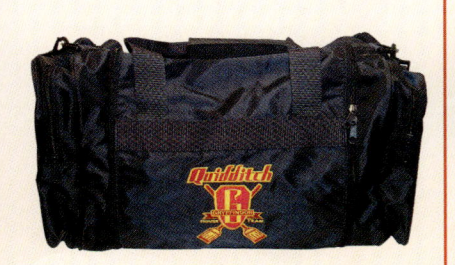

33
Quidditch Sports Bag
Bag • Retail: $24
Item #: HM223 • Issued: 2000

34
**Black Lightning Bolt Cap
(adult, one size fits most)**
Hat • Retail: $16
Item #: GM438 • Issued: 2000

Harry Potter Product Showcase

Warner Bros. Product Spotlight

Harry Potter Product Showcase

35
**Black Quidditch Hat
(kids', w/adjustable strap)**
Hat • Retail: $14
Item #: LA004 • Issued: 2000

36
**Navy Hogwarts Crest Cap
(adult, one size fits most)**
Hat • Retail: $16
Item #: GM437 • Issued: 2000

37
**Navy Quidditch Cap
(adult, one size fits most)**
Hat • Retail: $16
Item #: HM202 • Issued: 2000

38
Golden Snitch Keyring
Keyring • Retail: $4.50
Item #: GM465 • Issued: 2000

COLLECTOR'S
VALUE GUIDE™

Warner Bros. Product Spotlight

Harry Potter Product Showcase

39
Leather Strap Watch And Tin Set
Watch • Retail: N/A
Item #: N/A • Issued: 2000

40
Light Up Watch And Tin Set
Watch • Retail: $28
Item #: GM452 • Issued: 2000

41
Mood Watch And Tin Set (with ring)
Watch • Retail: N/A
Item #: N/A • Issued: 2000

42
Velvet Strap Watch And Tin Set
Watch • Retail: $28
Item #: GM453 • Issued: 2000

COLLECTOR'S VALUE GUIDE™

Warner Bros. Product Spotlight

Harry Potter Product Showcase

School Supplies

All students need the latest in school supplies! So, if your pen runs out of ink or your notebook is filled with "charm"ing notes, check out a Warner Bros. Studio Store near you to get Harry Potter pens and other items for your days in the classroom.

1
Lightning Bolt Binder
Binder • Retail: $12
Item #: GM565 • Issued: 2000

2
Set Of 3 Bookcovers
Bookcovers • Retail: $4
Item #: GM564 • Issued: 2000

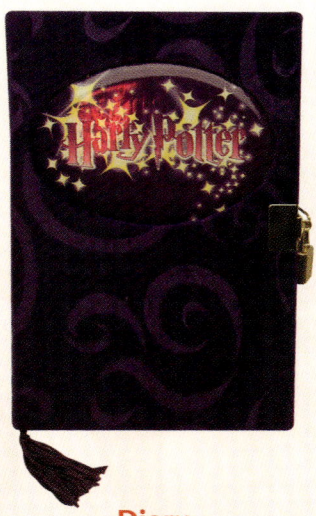

3
Diary
Diary • Retail: N/A
Item #: N/A • Issued: 2000

COLLECTOR'S VALUE GUIDE™

Warner Bros. Product Spotlight

4

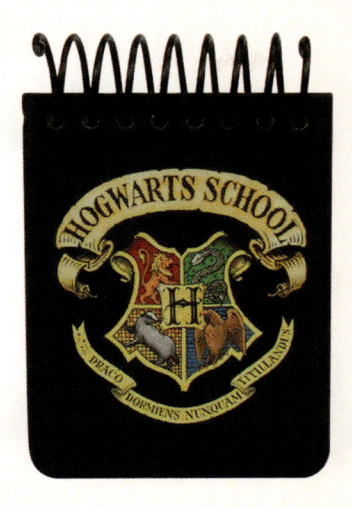

Hogwarts Logo Fat Book
Notebook • Retail: $3
Item #: GM556 • Issued: 2000

5

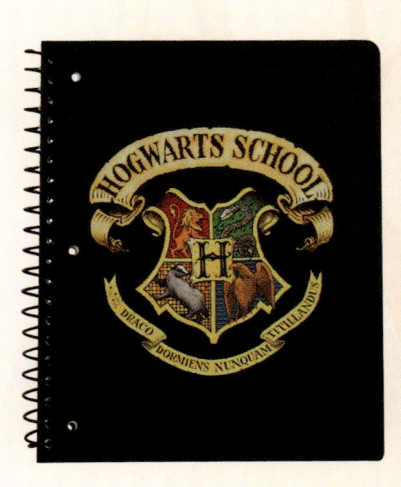

Hogwarts Spiral Notebook
Notebook • Retail: $4
Item #: SS837 • Issued: 2000

6

Set Of 6 Pens
Pens • Retail: $10
Item #: GM610 • Issued: 2000

Home Decor & Collectibles

Spruce up your home with these colorful Harry Potter items, including bookends, a picture frame and a clock. And for when the holidays approach, a snowglobe and two ornaments are available to help you decorate your "great hall!"

Harry Potter Product Showcase

COLLECTOR'S
VALUE GUIDE™

Harry Potter Product Showcase

Warner Bros. Product Spotlight

1

Platform 9 3/4 Bookends
Bookends • Retail: $30
Item #: GM568 • Issued: 2000

2

Desk Clock
Clock • Retail: $20
Item #: GM544 • Issued: 2000

3

Birth Of Norbert Mug
Mug • Retail: $8
Item #: NL106 • Issued: 2000

4

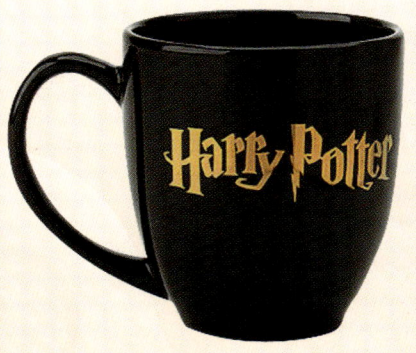

Harry Potter Logo Mug
Mug • Retail: $8
Item #: BM254 • Issued: 2000

COLLECTOR'S
VALUE GUIDE™

Warner Bros. Product Spotlight

5

6

Harry Potter With Flying Friends Mug
Mug • Retail: $8
Item #: NL104 • Issued: 2000

Hedwig Mug
Mug • Retail: $8
Item #: N/A • Issued: 2000

7

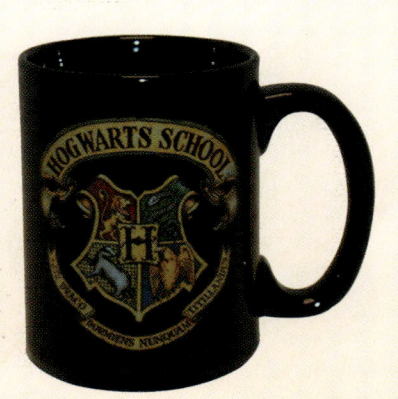

8

Hogwarts Crest Mug
Mug • Retail: $8
Item #: BM255 • Issued: 2000

Harry Potter On Nimbus 2000
Ornament • Retail: $10
Item #: N/A • Issued: 2000

Harry Potter Product Showcase

COLLECTOR'S
VALUE GUIDE™

Warner Bros. Product Spotlight

Harry Potter Product Showcase

9
Hedwig Messenger Owl
Ornament • Retail: $8
Item #: N/A • Issued: 2000

10
Picture Frame
Picture Frame • Retail: $18
Item #: GM570 • Issued: 2000

11
Hedwig
Plush • Retail: $16
Item #: N/A • Issued: 2000

12
Snowglobe
Snowglobe • Retail: $24
Item #: N/A • Issued: 2000

COLLECTOR'S VALUE GUIDE™

Warner Bros. Product Spotlight

Party Supplies

At this time, there are three items available at the Warner Bros. Studio Stores which are perfect for your next costume party. Wear the wizard robe, add a temporary tattoo on your forehead, put on the glasses and – poof! – you ARE Harry Potter!

1

Harry Potter Costume (kids' sizes only)
Costume • Retail: $24
Item #: HM161 • Issued: 2000

2

Harry's Glasses
Glasses • Retail: $4
Item #: HM186 • Issued: 2000

3

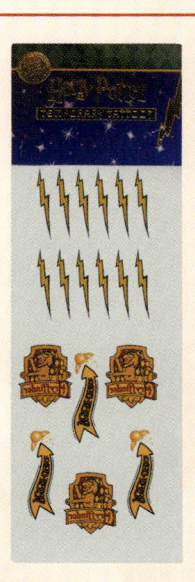

Temporary Tattoos
Tattoos • Retail: $3
Item #: HM195 • Issued: 2000

Harry Potter Product Showcase

Check our web site, CollectorsQuest.com, for new Warner Bros. Studio Store Harry Potter exclusives and record the information here.

Harry Potter Product Showcase

New Releases	Date Purch.	Price Paid	How Many	Total Value

A Magical Challenge

The rest of the *Harry Potter Product Showcase* will give you a sneak peek into the future at other Harry Potter merchandise coming soon to stores near you, beginning here with toys and games. Although Harry Potter has amazing powers that astound even experienced wizards, he *is* just a kid who likes to have fun. So, if you're like Harry and can't pass up a challenge, you will surely want to keep an eye on your local toy store so you don't miss any of the wonderful toys and games that are expected to be released in the coming months. For up-to-the minute news on Harry Potter-themed toys and games, make sure you log-on to www.CollectorsQuest.com.

Toys & Games

According to an eyewitness account, you will soon be able to fire-up your very own version of the Hogwarts Express. **Bachmann Trains** is licensed to produce Harry Potter model trains, so start building your own Platform Nine and Three-Quarters; you certainly wouldn't want to miss this opportunity to travel Harry Potter–style.

View-Masters have always been a favorite among kids, and you're certainly more likely to see something inside one of the upcoming **Fisher-Price, Inc.** View-Masters than in some of Professor Trelawney's murky crystal balls.

See Harry Potter's world through a View-Master by Fisher-Price.

Harry Potter Product Showcase

Flying Colors, a division of JAKKS Pacific Inc., will be developing Harry Potter craft and activity kits, according to *License!* magazine.

LEGO will soon be creating Harry Potter construction toy sets for kids ages 6-12. The first nine Harry Potter LEGO sets will be released in 2001, just before the release of the movie in the fall. In a press release, LEGO president and CEO Kjeld Kirk Kristiansen said "In the Harry Potter universe, everything is possible, and you never know what is going to happen next. This is exactly what happens when kids play with LEGO products; the only limit is their imagination."

You can build anything from Diagon Alley to Hogwarts with LEGOS.

The themes for the forthcoming LEGO sets have yet to be announced, but there are many intriguing places within the world of Harry Potter that you could imagine building with LEGOS including Hogwarts Castle, the bank Gringotts, the prison Azkaban or the Shrieking Shack in Hogsmeade.

Well-known toy manufacturer **Mattel** used a little sorcery of their own to ensure they were named the "master toy licensee" for the Harry Potter property. Mattel was so excited by the prospect of partnering with Warner Bros. that they reportedly had company executives dress in costume and present their ideas for products in rhyme in an attempt to win the rights to produce toys and games with Harry's likeness.

Hallmark's rendition of Gringotts in their "Gringotts™ Bank."

In a company press release, Matt Bousquette, President of Mattel's Boys and Entertainment division, says "... we are dedicated to ensuring that everything we create, from dolls and games to high-tech toys, will bring the characters to life in amazing new ways." A challenging Harry Potter trivia game is expected to arrive in stores in Fall 2000. Mattel will also produce action figures, puzzles and several other games. Many Mattel products will become available in selected stores in time for the 2000 holiday season.

Hallmark's "Quidditch" 100-Piece Sticker Puzzle" comes with two sheets of repositionable stickers.

Schylling, known for its line of tin toys, will be producing Harry Potter wind-up toys just in time for the holidays. Kids of all ages will be thrilled to receive a Schylling toy. Look for them at specialty and gift stores near you!

Toy Biz, the well-known producer of collectible action figures, is set to launch a line of Harry Potter inspired kites in the Summer of 2001. What better time to go fly a kite?

Board game manufacturer **University Games** has announced the release of two games and four 250-piece puzzles featuring Harry Potter. The "Harry Potter & The Sorcerer's Stone Game" features "6-3/4" games to choose from, while "Harry Potter's Quidditch Game" is based on Harry Potter's favorite sport, where players shoot a "Quaffle" through hoops to score and attempt to catch the sneaky "Golden Snitch."

"Harry Potter's Magic Puzzle" features lenticular pieces with images that appear to move, and the remaining three puzzles have a "glow in the dark" feature that offers a magical surprise when the lights are turned off. The first University Games products will first be available in specialty stores beginning in late October 2000.

Collectible card games have been making a big splash among kids lately, so it's exciting news that **Wizards of the Coast** of Renton, Washington – the makers of the Pokémon™ and Magic: The Gathering® trading card games – will be working their magic on a Harry Potter card game and other role-playing products.

These collectible cards by Wizards of the Coast are a natural choice, since Harry Potter's fictional wizard world also features a set of collectible cards, called "Famous Witches and Wizards," which are packaged with Chocolate Frogs. In *Harry Potter and the Sorcerer's Stone,* these cards are introduced to Harry on the Hogwarts Express when Ron tells him that he has a collection of around 500 of these magical cards.

This chocolate frog and "Famous Witches And Wizards" card were trade show promotional items given away by Warner Bros.

ELECTRONICS

Electronic Arts™ of Redwood City, California will be creating Harry Potter video, computer and Internet games. In an August 2000 article in Great Britain's *Telegraph*, Bruce McMillan, managing director of Electronic Arts' European studios, marvels at the interactive possibilities associated with the Harry Potter storylines. He predicted that Electronic Arts' games will explore secrets in Hogwarts Castle, the Forbidden Forest and characters based on the writing of J. K. Rowling.

Most of us "non-wizard" types rely on technological wizards to bring magic into our lives and **Tiger Electronics** of Vernon Hills, Illinois will be doing just that with its Harry Potter product line. A division of toy giant Hasbro, Tiger Electronics will be releasing hand-held electronic games, personal radios and recorders, diaries, children's messaging systems and voice changing devices. Hasbro chairman and CEO Alan G. Hassenfeld promises in a press release "to bring the magic [of Harry Potter] into new and exciting worlds."

Now that you have passed the magical challenge and have stocked up on Harry Potter toys and games, how about some Potter-themed clothing and accessories? Read on to find out what is coming in the world of Harry Potter apparel!

A Wizard's Wardrobe

Everyone will want to keep up with the latest Harry Potter fashions – and you'll be able to find plenty at a Madam Malkin's Robes for All Occasions shop near you. The first wave of licensed apparel began appearing in Warner Bros. stores in late summer 2000, but many more products will be released in a wide variety of retail outlets after December 26, 2000. An additional wave of merchandise is expected to hit stores about eight weeks before the Fall 2001 release of the first Harry Potter movie. Stay tuned to www.CollectorsQuest.com for forthcoming Harry Potter apparel.

Wear your school pride with Tri-Star's and Starline Creations' "Gryffindor" ring.

T-Shirts, Tops & Sleepwear

Adorable Kids Inc. of Montreal, Quebec, in Canada, will produce a line of boys' sleepwear that, when partnered with a hot mug of butterbeer, is sure to keep any budding wizard warm during cold, winter nights. The line is expected to be released in Spring 2001.

Before taking on Harry Potter boys' and men's T-shirts, **Changes** featured licensed products for another famous Potter in the literary world – Beatrix Potter™. Pat the Bunny™ and Maisy® round out the company's lineup of children's book licensees.

This "Hogwarts Crest" T-shirt can be found at Warner Bros. Studio Stores.

Harry, who demonstrated his musical skills through playing the flute to Fluffy in *Harry Potter and the Sorcerer's Stone*, became the latest musician to work with Los Angeles based **Giant Merchandising**. Other famous musical clients include Aerosmith, Metallica and The Smashing Pumpkins. Giant has a license to manufacture Potter-themed T-shirts and tops for both men and boys, which will be available in mass market stores around the country.

Monterey Canyon Apparel will also produce Harry Potter T-shirts and tops for the boys' and men's categories which will be sold in mass market and department stores.

Sportswear & Swimwear

Whether it's soccer, baseball, basketball or any number of sports, kids (and adults!) everywhere can relate to Harry Potter's passion for the magical sport of Quidditch. And the athletically-inclined will have no shortage of Harry Potter apparel to wear during their active endeavors.

If you are chosen to participate in your school's team for the next Triwizard Tournament, you may want to purchase some of the sportswear and swimwear that will be manufactured by **Happy Kids.** Whether your challenge is swimming in the school's lake or running through a maze, Happy Kids has an outfit for every event and activity.

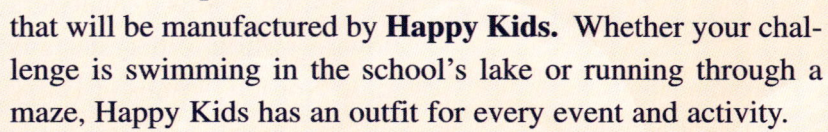

Isaac Morris' Harry Potter product line will focus on boys' separates (pants, shirts, etc., though they have no immediate plans for Weasley sweaters) in sizes 8-16, which will be available in department stores such as Sears and JCPenney.

Jerry Leigh Entertainment Apparel of Los Angeles is known for producing a wide variety of licensed apparel, including tops, sweaters, dresses and more. Jerry Leigh has been licensed to produce sportswear and tops for juniors and girls.

Multiprint Manufacturing, a division of the Canadian corporation Multigroup, will produce boys' outerwear (jackets, though presumably no Invisibility Cloaks!) and girls' activewear (T-shirts, etc.) in Fall 2001. Their line of boys' and girls' swimwear is expected in Spring 2002.

Novel Teez Designs (NTD) Apparel Inc. was awarded a license for boys' swimwear and denim in Canada. The products are expected to be in selected stores by January 2001.

SOCKS, BOXERS & BRIEFS

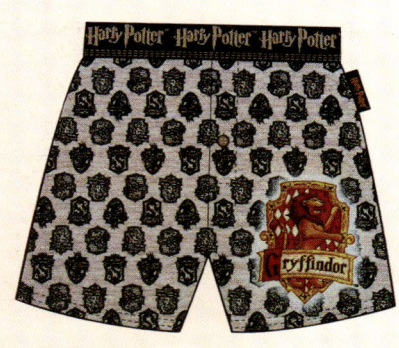

Boxer short and pajama manufacturer **Briefly Stated** has plans to release an initial 10 styles of boxer shorts based on the Harry Potter novels. Designs include "Harry Chasing The Snitch" and "Scabbers Allover," while other designs feature Norbert, scenes of Harry in different activities and a crest of Gryffindor. The first wave of six products will be available in January 2001, while a second set will make their way to stores in March 2001.

An artist's rendition from Briefly Stated of boxer shorts that will be available in early 2001.

The socks and tights made by New York manufacturer **High Point** are sure to be the perfect accessory for keeping warm (and quiet!) when sneaking around the dungeons at night. The products will make their debut in January 2001 to upscale markets, while the anticipated mass-market release will be eight weeks before the movie opens.

Sara Max, which was renamed in 1998 after six years as Intimate Resources, Inc., plans to release new lines of both boys' and girls' Harry Potter-themed underwear.

Put you best foot forward with socks from High Point. The sock shown here is an artist's rendition from the company.

RAINWEAR

Quidditch matches are rarely delayed for inclement weather so, whether you're sitting in the stands or playing on the field, you may want to stock up on some of the Harry Potter rainwear, zipper pulls and headwear which will soon be available from **Berkshire Rainwear**.

In Spring 2001, **Totes Isotoner** expects to release its line of raincoats and umbrellas for kids, in addition to umbrellas for adults. The products will be available in specialty stores and department stores. Totes Isotoner is planning to pull out lots of magical tricks with its Harry Potter line, including special lights and secret compartments. Harlan Kent, senior vice president of Totes Isotoner was quoted as saying, "When you hit the button on an umbrella, we can do all kinds of magical imagery."

Bags

If you're looking for a place to store your books, your magic wand or even your brand-new broomstick, **Accessory Network** will be releasing bags in the spring of 2001. The bags come in all styles and shapes, including four plush backpacks shaped as Hedwig the owl, the Sorting Hat, the Golden Snitch and a Winged Potion. In addition to the bags, Accessory Network has plans to release both small and large novelty banks and tins, in addition to skid-free slippers, which feature special pads on the bottom to reduce slipping. According to an article in *Brandweek*, the products could feature "elements like magic wands and pockets with surprises in them," although details haven't yet been finalized.

Tuck your school supplies into a "Ravenclaw Backpack" by Accessory Network

Jaclyn, Inc. will feature a large selection of Harry Potter products that any Hogwarts student would love, such as denim backpacks, totebags, handbags, wallets, keyrings and cosmetic bags. The first wave of products, which will be produced in six different kinds of denim including cross-died denim, sparkle denim, diesel denim and Timberland denim, will be available in specialty stores at the end of December 2000. The products will be available through mass-market channels around the back-to-school season in 2001.

Keep your cash safe in wallets and coin purses from Jaclyn, Inc.

Watches And Jewelry

If you don't have a "Time-Turner" hourglass like Hermione in *Harry Potter and the Prisoner of Azkaban*, you might want a Harry Potter watch to get you to all of your lessons (or meetings) on time. **Fossil** has been producing watches since 1984 and its product line includes popular licensed characters such as Snoopy and Spider-Man.

Watches from Fossil are packaged in an attractive and useful tin box.

Tri-Star Merchandise and **Starline Creations** pair up to produce a line of jewelry and accessories based on Harry Potter and his adventures. Pendants, lightning bolt-shaped pins, and rings featuring the crests of the four different Hogwarts houses are among the designs to be released. Bracelets, charm necklaces and musical jewelry boxes will also be available.

Pendant from Tri-Star Merchandise and Starline Creations.

Sunglasses

Sunglasses have always been hip and the bespectacled Harry Potter has brought eyewear to a whole new level of cool. **Pan Oceanic Eyewear** will be releasing approximately 30 styles of sunglasses on December 26, 2000. According to *License!* magazine, the company is also licensed to make cases and cords. Pan Oceanic Eyewear's products can be found at most major department stores, including Kmart, Wal-Mart, Target and Sears, among others.

Back To School

Harry Potter is no ordinary kid and that's not just because of his other-worldly powers. Have you noticed how much he can't wait to get back to school? (It may, however, have something to do with his living arrangements during the summer!) Probably the only thing scarier than heading back to school is heading back to school unprepared. But if you're not like Harry and would rather have an endless summer, why not soften the blow of returning to class by stocking up on loads of Harry Potter merchandise to satisfy all of your school supply needs.

These pens are available at the Warner Bros. Studio Stores and come in a set of six.

Address Books, Photo Albums & More

Cedco Publishing of San Rafael, California, has been licensed to produce colorful Harry Potter address books, sticker books, photo albums and other fun activity products. According to Cedco, their first Harry Potter products – 18 varieties in all – should become available by early November 2000. Cedco will have three address book designs that will appeal to all kinds of fans; a Harry Potter theme, a Hermione Granger theme and a "suede-lux" address book for adults. A "Remembrall Memory Book" from Cedco will be available for recording all of life's activities, though it probably won't be magical like Tom Riddle's diary in *Harry Potter and the Chamber of Secrets*.

You won't need a password to open one of Cedco's new photo albums, but if you provide your own sorcery, maybe the pictures will move like they do in Harry's leather-bound photo album that Hagrid gave him. The three photo albums that will be released are sure to please any fan as they will have a choice of covers featuring either the Hogwarts Crest, the Mirror of Erised or Harry Potter.

The themes for Cedco's "Big Sticker Books" will be Harry Potter, Hermione, Hogwarts and Quidditch. For those on the go, there are six unique backpack books, each designed for different record-keeping activities – two for photos and one each for autographs, addresses, web sites and friends. Any dedicated student will love to get their very own "Harry Potter Student Planner," which can help organize your schedule from August 2000 to December 2001.

BANDAGES & TOILETRIES

Students at Hogwarts are constantly getting banged up and end up having to spend a lot of time in the hospital wing of the school. Right now, they depend on the school nurse, Madam Pomfrey, to heal their myriad of ailments and injuries, but in the future they may look to **Johnson & Johnson** products. According to *License!* magazine, Johnson & Johnson is licensed to produce bandages, toiletries and oral care products for children.

Calendars

Harry Potter is always looking ahead to something, whether it's an upcoming Quidditch match or the extravagant Halloween festivities. The time of year that a new calendar is especially important to Harry is during the summer, as he counts down the days to a new school year at Hogwarts.

Andrews McMeel is well-known for publishing fine books and calendars and will be producing a number of Harry Potter products including two calendars which are expected to arrive in select department stores and bookstores by November 2000. You can choose from a colorful wall calendar or a "day-to-day" desk calendar.

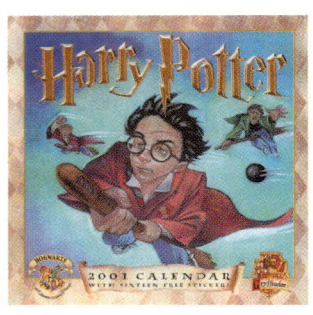

This attractive wall calendar from Andrews McMeel comes with 16 free stickers!

Lunch Kits

As you know, when Harry Potter returns to school, he fills his lunch box with chocolate frogs and all sorts of magical treats. **Thermos**® is planning to release Harry Potter lunch kits in the summer of 2001, right in time for next year's back-to-school rush. Thermos' products can be found in most drug stores, such as CVS and Walgreen's, and department stores.

Carry your rock cakes and butterbeer in Hallmark's *Harry Potter and the Sorcerer's Stone* Numbered Limited Edition Lunch Box."

Pens, Journals & More

Certainly, the popularity of J. K. Rowling's books will inspire many kids to take up writing and, even in these days of technological wizardry, the pen remains a symbol for aspiring writers. **Hallmark** has many Harry Potter products that are perfect for the school or office, including "light-up" pens, pen and paper gift sets, lenticular journals and diaries and even a lunch box. The first six pen designs feature lightning bolts, Quidditch balls, Norbert the dragon and Bertie Bott's Every Flavor Beans, among others. Two additional pen designs are scheduled to arrive in stores in December 2000, one featuring the snowy owl Hedwig and the other with the Hogwarts Crest.

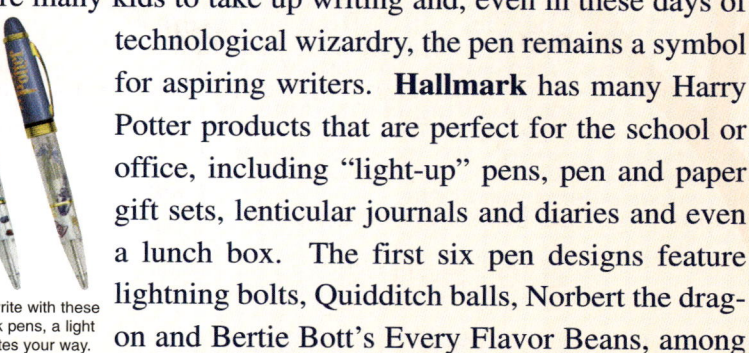

As you write with these Hallmark pens, a light illuminates your way.

Rubber Stamps

According to *License!* magazine, **All Night Media** will be producing stickers and rubber stampers. The company currently features a prolific line of rubber stamps, including designs featuring Curious George®, Dr. Seuss™ and Mary Engelbreit®.

Back To School In 2001

You can expect a lot of great back-to-school merchandise to be released before the next school year begins. Be sure to check www.CollectorsQuest.com for the latest information on Harry Potter school supplies.

Through The Picture Frame

From the Gryffindor House to your house, everyone loves decorating. You can select from among many forthcoming Harry Potter accessories to spruce up any room! You can expect a lot more exciting Harry Potter home decor products to be released soon, so to keep up-to-date, stay tuned to **www.CollectorsQuest.com**.

Bed, Bath & The Beach

Nothing makes Harry Potter happier than arriving back at Hogwarts School and seeing his familiar bedroom that's full of four-poster beds. Maybe if he surrounds his bed with some of the soon-to-be-released Harry Potter bedding products, he can help keep the "bad guys" away!

According to *License!* magazine, **Crown Crafts**, based in Atlanta, Georgia, will be creating a line of Harry Potter throws and pillows.

Franco Manufacturing expects their line of Harry Potter bedding and towels to be available in department stores and other select retailers in early 2001.

Sunbathing is made even more fun with this "Quidditch" beach towel from TerriSol.

Producer of bed and bath products and other coordinated home fashions, **Springs Industries** has been licensed to create a variety of home furnishings, which includes bedding, area rugs and bath accessories. Torrence Shealy, the company's senior vice president for marketing, states in a press release that Springs will be producing "a complete Harry Potter fantasy ensemble." The company's products will first be available in Warner Bros. Studio Stores during the 2000 holiday season, and will later become available at select department and specialty stores. A mass-market release is planned for July 2001. Moaning Myrtle is sure to be delighted with the variety of choices available if she decides to decorate her bathroom!

The TerriSol "Flying Keys" beach towel is a great holiday gift.

TerriSol Corp. of New York has released their first seven Harry Potter beach towel designs, which will make their debut in Warner Bros. Studio Stores in October 2000. The products will later be available in fine department stores, bed and bath retailers and bookstores. The towels are 30" x 60" and feature action-packed scenes inspired by the first book in the series, *Harry Potter and the Sorcerer's Stone*. The book's major characters of Harry Potter, Ron Weasley and Hermione Granger are well-represented on TerriSol's towels while there are also exciting renditions of other characters like Hagrid, creepy Professor Snape and the ferocious, three-headed dog, Fluffy.

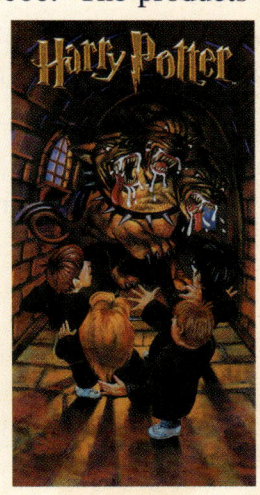

Too bad the real Fluffy isn't as soft and furry as this beach towel by TerriSol.

HOME DECOR & COLLECTIBLES

Based in New York, the **Alexander Doll Company**, producer of collectible Madame Alexander® dolls, plans to produce Harry Potter products which will be available mid-2001. Currently, the Alexander Doll Company is featuring lines of collectibles based on the characters of Stuart Little™ and Eloise™, in addition to the Wicked Witch, Dorothy and others from the classic tale *The Wizard of Oz*™.

Place Department 56's "Harry Potter™" on your mantle.

If you don't remember the password to your vault in the wizard bank, Gringotts, you can store your valuables in one of six Secret Boxes™ produced by **Department 56® Inc.** The boxes feature the Golden Snitch and the Sorting Hat, in addition to showcasing characters such as Harry, Hermione, Hagrid and Hedwig. The company will also produce a "Harry Potter Animated Scene" which features Harry flying high on his broom.

Several mug designs from **Encore/Xpres**® became available in Warner Bros. Studio Stores in Fall 2000, with scenes

Beverages will be so much tastier in this mug from Encore/Xpres.

such as Hedwig the owl winking and Harry Potter riding his broomstick. Fill these with some yummy butterbeer or even some of Professor Snape's potions – if you dare.

Harry Potter's friend, Ron Weasley, has shown a tendency to collect figurines – he purchased one of the Quidditch player, Viktor Krum, while attending the Quidditch World Cup in *Harry Potter and the Goblet of Fire*. A leader in the gift and collectibles market, the **Enesco Group, Inc.** of Itasca, Illinois is licensed to create a variety of Harry Potter products including collectible "Storyteller" and mini figurines. Additionally, there is a wide variety of bookends, collector stones and more.

Ron Weasley is poised and ready to create magic in this Enesco Mini Figurine.

Fetco International of Randolph, Massachusetts will be releasing a wide variety of Harry Potter photo frames, albums and storage boxes, framed wall mirrors and other photo display items. The first products will be available in select retailers in early 2001 and more products will be released to the mass market in Fall 2001. In a press release, the company's president, John Whoriskey, cited Fetco's "innovative design capabilities" as being a key to the excitement over the forthcoming Harry Potter product line. Perhaps Fetco's photo frames should have enhanced security features to prevent the pictures from running away like the framed and fearful fat lady who guards the Gryffindor House in *Harry Potter and the Prisoner of Azkaban*!

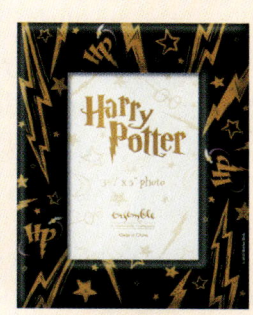

Photo frames are a very unique part of Harry's wizard world. Both Fetco and Hallmark (shown here) will be producing Harry Potter photo frames.

Famous for their teddy bears and stuffed animals, plush manufacturer, **Gund**®, anticipates creating five Harry Potter items for early 2001, with more to follow. Gund's products will be available in gift and department stores as well as bookstores.

In addition to their many other Harry Potter items, **Hallmark** will release four pewter Keepsake Ornaments. A set of six Harry Potter-themed charms will also be available. And to really show your Harry Potter pride, you may want to display Hallmark's hanging fabric "Hogwarts™ Crest" in your room.

With six "Hogwarts™ Charms" by Hallmark, there is a charm for every mood.

Framed art, canvas and shadow boxes will be produced by licensee **Intercontinental Art,** who plans to announce details about their merchandise in October 2000.

Kurt S. Adler will offer an assortment of beautiful Christmas ornaments – including resin, tin, glass ball, blow mold and Polonaise ornaments. Can you imagine these wonderful ornaments sparkling in the trees on the grounds of Hogwarts during the gala Yule Ball? The company will also offer a light set featuring Harry playing his favorite game of Quidditch and a holiday stocking.

"Harry With Wand And Hedwig" from Kurt S. Adler will fly right onto your holiday tree.

P. J. Kids®, specializes in juvenile furniture and expects to announce its Harry Potter product line in October 2000. Perhaps there will be a table and set of chairs where we can sit and enjoy celebrations with a Harry Potter theme. Read on to find out more about Potter party possibilities!

The Neverending Feast

You're invited to celebrate any occasion in a distinctly Harry Potter theme. Despite the dangers which seem to constantly lurk around Hogwarts School, the students always find time to celebrate in a big way. The school's Great Hall is always extravagantly decorated for various occasions like Halloween, Christmas or the Triwizard Tournament. And a hard-fought Quidditch victory often inspires the winning "house" to throw a boisterous celebration.

Cakes & Candy

Bring on the cake! In the summer between his third and fourth years at Hogwarts, Harry Potter secretly feasted on four birthday cakes sent by his friends, while the rest of the Dursley household suffered through a strict vegetable-and-fruit diet designed to control Dudley's weight. Now you can enjoy cake too, as both **DecoPac** and **Wilton Industries** will be creating Harry Potter cake-decorating kits and supplies, perfect for your own Harry Potter–themed party.

Hasbro's **OddzOn** division will be producing Harry Potter candy through its Cap Candy division. The first scheduled release will be the famous "Bertie Bott's Every Flavor Beans," inspired by the popular and unusual candy in the Harry Potter books. While the more extreme flavors like booger and tripe will not be included (for now, anyway), fans

Tri-Star Merchandise has produced a coin purse with a Bertie Bott's Every Flavor Beans theme.

will find a variety of unusual flavors, from sardine and baked bean to grass and black pepper. Look out for other flavors included in the books, such as toast, coconut, strawberry, curry, coffee, spinach, liver, sprouts and more. Cap Candy is also expected to release a line of spin pops based on the popular book series.

Tri-Star Merchandise has also produced a jewelry box featuring the popular candy.

Hats & Costumes

Elope has introduced eight fanciful Harry Potter hat designs for the fashionable party animal. Fans of the books can choose from designs including: Harry's owl, Hedwig; Ron's rat, Scabbers; and Argus Filch's cat, Mrs. Norris. If you'd rather look like a wizard, you can choose from the Sorting Hat, Harry Potter's hat or Professor Gilderoy Lockhart's hat. To top it all off, Elope will be releasing a pair of official Harry Potter glasses, which appear to have been freshly repaired by "Spellotape" after a brutal Quidditch match.

The annual Halloween feast is always a treat at the Hogwarts School, although most of those ghosts aren't wearing costumes! Next Halloween, many kids will surely choose their costumes from among **Rubie's Costumes'** Harry Potter designs. Beware, anyone could be Lord Voldemort – er, "You-Know-Who" – in disguise!

The more heads the better with this "Fluffy" hat from Elope.

PARTY SUPPLIES

So, you've been invited to Nearly Headless Nick's "deathday" party celebrating the 500th anniversary of his death and you still haven't wrapped the gift or gotten a card? Well then you'd better "apparate" down to your local **Hallmark** store. Hallmark will debut its Harry Potter products in mid-October 2000. Among the offerings are several items that will enhance any party, including gift wrap, greeting cards and "party ware." In a press release, Greg Raymond, marketing director of Hallmark Licensing, says, "Harry Potter fans will find Hallmark has stayed true to the characters in the book series and has found ways to incorporate features that will make those products truly special." Let's hope that Hallmark's line doesn't extend to "Howlers," special eardrum-shattering messages sent in anger in the wizard world!

Hallmark's Pen And Paper Gift Set makes a wonderful "deathday" present.

M&D Industries will be introducing Harry Potter mylar balloons in November 2000. This Illinois-based company has been producing metallic balloons since 1978 and holds licenses for Winnie the Pooh and Rugrats among others.

Parties are fun no matter what, but with the help of Harry Potter, they can be simply "bewitching!"

This curly cascade from Hallmark is the perfect topping for any present.

How To Use Your Collector's Value Guide™

1. The *Value Guide* section for Harry Potter books begins on the next page. The British versions are listed first in chronological order, followed by the United States versions. Each book is listed with its release date, format available, retail price and secondary market value in U.S. dollars. Values for uncorrected proofs ("Proof") and advance reading copies ("Advance") are sometimes given. (Note: the retail price given for the audio format is for compact discs.) The British and U.S books are followed by an alphabetical listing of the 30 other languages the Harry Potter series has been translated into so far.

2. The *Collectibles Showcase* section for other Harry Potter collectibles begins on page 119, which is organized alphabetically by manufacturer. *The retail prices given are likely price ranges and are subject to change. Keep in mind that some products pictured were still awaiting product approvals and may be prototypes or drawings. Actual production pieces may vary.*

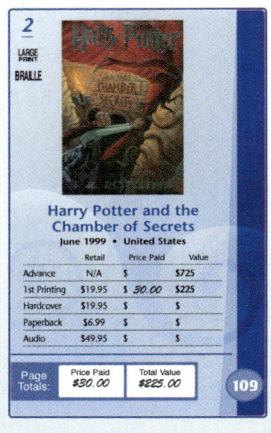

3. Record the price that you paid for each item in the spaces provided. Secondary market values are provided for first printings of the U.K. and U.S. versions of the books. For other book editions and in the *Collectibles Showcase* section, there is space left to fill in the current market value, which is usually the price you paid. To follow the emerging Harry Potter secondary market, check in regularly to **www.CollectorsQuest.com**.

4. Add the "price paid" for your items and write the total in the boxes at the bottom of each page. Then do the same with the values.

5. Transfer the totals of each page to the fill-in section on pages 161-162. Add the totals together to determine the overall value of your collection. Use a pencil so you can change the totals as your collection grows!

Value Guide – Harry Potter

The Books

The Harry Potter series of books has reached amazing heights of popularity. The phenomenon began with the publication of the first book in Great Britain in June of 1997 and has continued with the publication of three more so far. With three more books still to come, there's no telling how much bigger the Harry Potter phenomenon will become.

Harry has conquered the world and is being published internationally in a variety of languages and formats. The British and American books are available in several formats including hardcover, paperback and audio. Braille and large print editions are denoted by icons in this section. In Great Britain, the books are available with many covers, including deluxe and adult editions.

British Editions

Before Harry Potter came to the United States, he was a big hit in Great Britain. The first editions of the first three books were released in Great Britain and command a high secondary market value. First printings of *Harry Potter and the Philosopher's Stone* are especially rare since only 300 were printed.

1 Harry Potter and the Philosopher's Stone
June 1997 • Great Britain

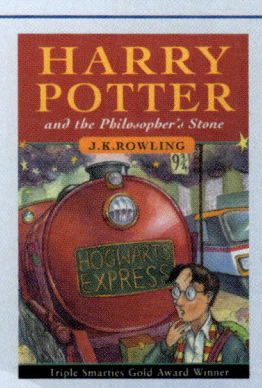

	Retail	Price Paid	Value
Proof	N/A	$	$14,000
1st Printing	£10.99	$	$23,500
Hardcover	£10.99	$	$
Paperback	£5.99	$	$
Audio	£37.99	$	$

Page Totals: | Price Paid | Total Value |

The Books

Value Guide – Harry Potter

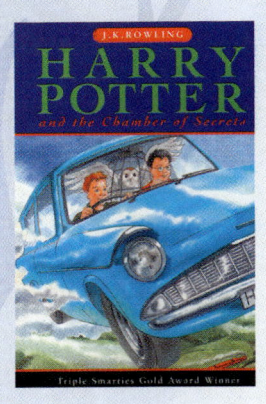

2
Harry Potter and the Chamber of Secrets
July 1998 • Great Britain

	Retail	Price Paid	Value
1st Printing	£10.99	$	$3,000
Hardcover	£10.99	$	$
Paperback	£5.99	$	$
Audio	£42.99	$	$

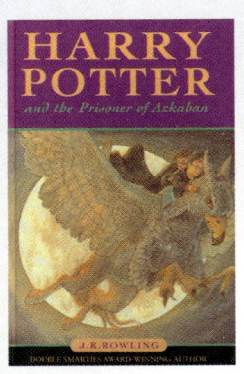

3
Harry Potter and the Prisoner of Azkaban
July 1999 • Great Britain

	Retail	Price Paid	Value
1st Print./© Joanne	£10.99	$	$1,500
1st Print./© J. K.	£10.99	$	$290
Hardcover	£10.99	$	$
Paperback	£5.99	$	$
Audio	£52.99	$	$

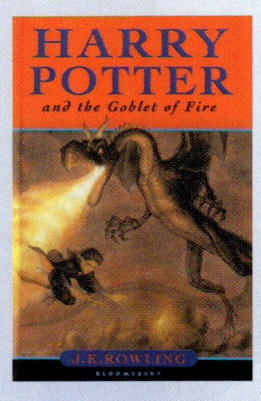

4
Harry Potter and the Goblet of Fire
July 2000 • Great Britain

	Retail	Price Paid	Value
1st Printing	£14.99	$	$85
Hardcover	£14.99	$	$
Paperback	£5.99	$	$
Audio	£44.99	$	$

British Adult Editions

Everyone knows that the Harry Potter series is popular with children, but many don't realize that adults everywhere have been secretly reading the series too. As a result, Bloomsbury has released the books with cover art meant to appeal to an older crowd.

Page Totals: Price Paid | Total Value

COLLECTOR'S VALUE GUIDE™

Value Guide – Harry Potter

The Books

1

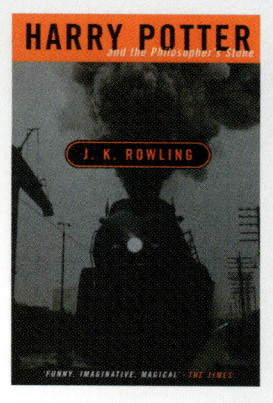

Harry Potter and the Philosopher's Stone
September 1998 • Great Britain

	Retail	Price Paid	Value
1st Printing	£6.99	$	N/E
Paperback	£6.99	$	$
Audio	£37.99	$	$

2

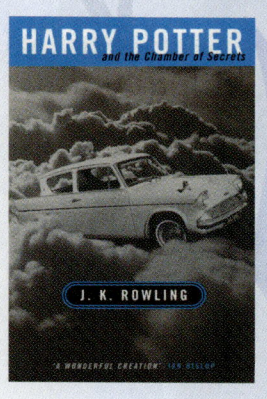

Harry Potter and the Chamber of Secrets
July 1999 • Great Britain

	Retail	Price Paid	Value
1st Printing	£6.99	$	N/E
Paperback	£6.99	$	$
Audio	£42.99	$	$

3

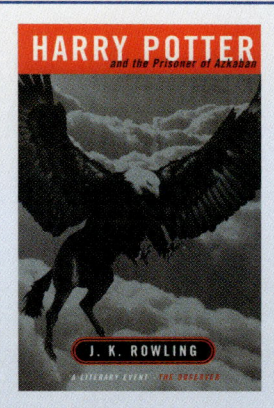

Harry Potter and the Prisoner of Azkaban
April 2000 • Great Britain

	Retail	Price Paid	Value
1st Printing	£6.99	$	N/E
Paperback	£6.99	$	$
Audio	£26.99*	$	$

only cassette price available at time of printing

4

Coming Soon

Harry Potter and the Goblet of Fire
April 2001 • Great Britain

	Retail	Price Paid	Value
1st Printing	£6.99	$	$
Paperback	£6.99	$	$
Audio	N/A	$	$

Page Totals: Price Paid | Total Value

COLLECTOR'S VALUE GUIDE™

Value Guide – Harry Potter

British Deluxe Editions

British Deluxe Editions have been published for each of the books. While the inside text remains the same as the other editions, these books feature special cloth covers with J. K. Rowling's signature stamped in gold, gilt-edged pages and a sewn-in bookmark.

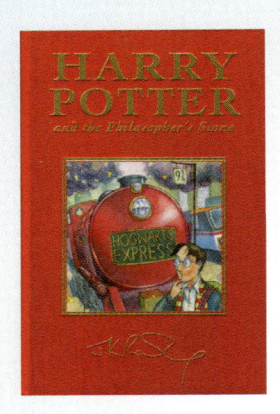

1

Harry Potter and the Philosopher's Stone
1999 • Great Britain

	Retail	Price Paid	Value
1st Printing	£18	$	$300
Hardcover	£18	$	$

2

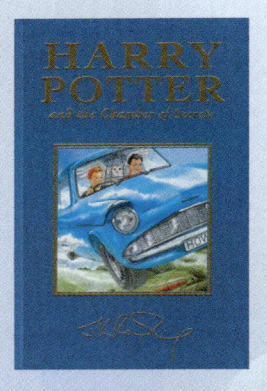

Harry Potter and the Chamber of Secrets
1999 • Great Britain

	Retail	Price Paid	Value
1st Printing	£18	$	$150
Hardcover	£18	$	$

3

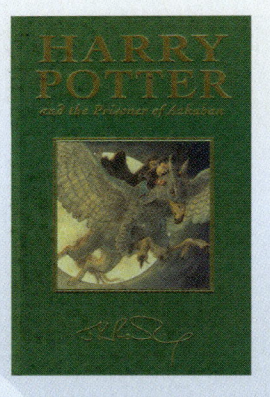

Harry Potter and the Prisoner of Azkaban
1999 • Great Britain

	Retail	Price Paid	Value
1st Printing	£18	$	$1,000
Hardcover	£18	$	$

Page Totals: Price Paid | Total Value

COLLECTOR'S VALUE GUIDE™

Value Guide – Harry Potter

4

Coming Soon

Harry Potter and the Goblet of Fire
October 2000 • Great Britain

	Retail	Price Paid	Value
1st Printing	£25	$	N/E
Hardcover	£25	$	$

U.S. Editions

When Harry Potter finally landed in the United States in October of 1998, he made a big splash – *Harry Potter and the Sorcerer's Stone* was an immediate best seller. These books, published by Scholastic, differ from the British versions with new cover art, interior chapter illustrations and Americanized vocabulary.

1
LARGE PRINT
BRAILLE

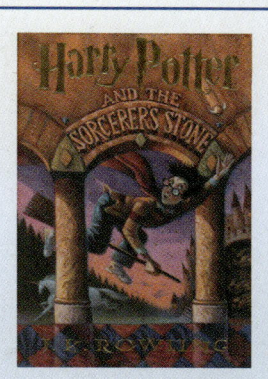

Harry Potter and the Sorcerer's Stone
October 1998 • United States

	Retail	Price Paid	Value
Advance	N/A	$	$2,700
1st Printing	$19.95	$	$5,700
Hardcover	$19.95	$	$
Paperback	$6.99	$	$
Audio	$49.95	$	$

2
LARGE PRINT
BRAILLE

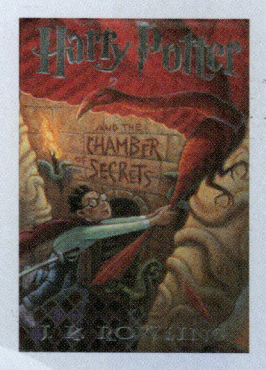

Harry Potter and the Chamber of Secrets
June 1999 • United States

	Retail	Price Paid	Value
Advance	N/A	$	$725
1st Printing	$19.95	$	$225
Hardcover	$19.95	$	$
Paperback	$6.99	$	$
Audio	$49.95	$	$

COLLECTOR'S VALUE GUIDE™

Page Totals: | Price Paid | Total Value

Value Guide – Harry Potter

3 LARGE PRINT BRAILLE

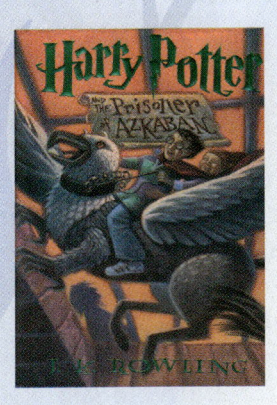

Harry Potter and the Prisoner of Azkaban
October 1999 • United States

	Retail	Price Paid	Value
Advance	N/A	$	**$540**
1st Printing	$19.95	$	**$175**
Hardcover	$19.95	$	$
Audio	$54.95	$	$

4

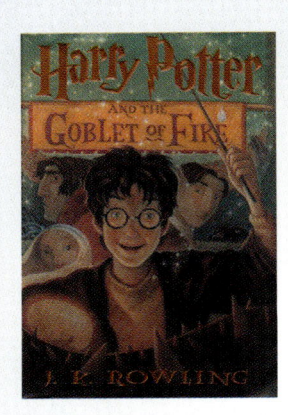

Harry Potter and the Goblet of Fire
July 2000 • United States

	Retail	Price Paid	Value
Advance	N/A	$	N/E
1st Printing	$25.95	$	**$80**
Hardcover	$25.95	$	$
Audio	$69.95	$	$

Page Totals: Price Paid / Total Value

COLLECTOR'S VALUE GUIDE™

Value Guide – Harry Potter

International Books

Harry Potter has not only crossed the seas to the United States, he has also journeyed to over 100 foreign countries. Published in over 30 languages, the series of books can be read just about anywhere in the world. (*Books noted with an asterisk (*) are not pictured.*)

1

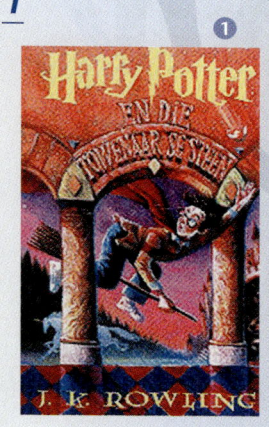

Afrikaans

	Price Paid	Value
Book 1	$	$
Book 2	$	$
Book 3	$	$

2

Bahasa Indonesian

	Price Paid	Value
Book 1*	$	$

3

Bulgarian

	Price Paid	Value
Book 1*	$	$
Book 2*	$	$

COLLECTOR'S VALUE GUIDE™

Page Totals:	Price Paid	Total Value

111

Value Guide – Harry Potter

International Books

4

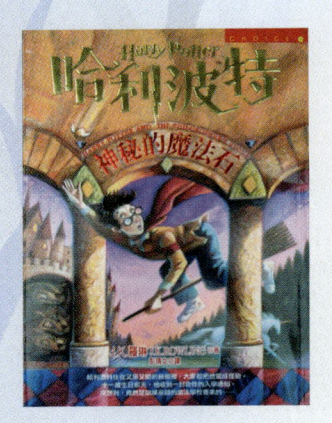

Chinese

	Price Paid	Value
Book 1	$	$

5

Photo Unavailable

Croatian

	Price Paid	Value
Book 1*	$	$
Book 2*	$	$

6

Photo Unavailable

Czechoslovakian

	Price Paid	Value
Book 1*	$	$
Book 2*	$	$

7

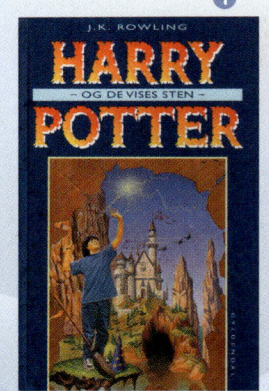

❶ ❷ ❸

Danish

	Price Paid	Value
Book 1	$	$
Book 2	$	$
Book 3	$	$

Page Totals: Price Paid ___ Total Value ___

COLLECTOR'S VALUE GUIDE™

Value Guide – Harry Potter

8

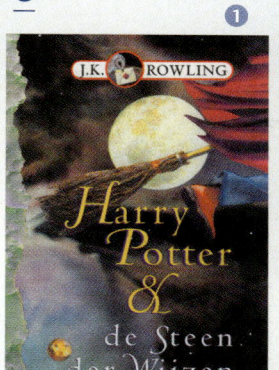

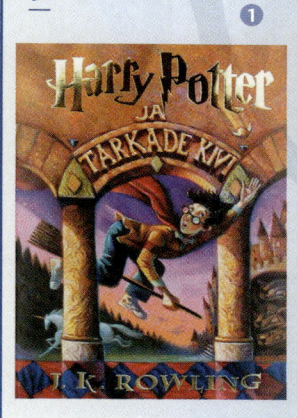

Dutch

	Price Paid	Value
Book 1	$	$
Book 2	$	$
Book 3	$	$

9

Estonian

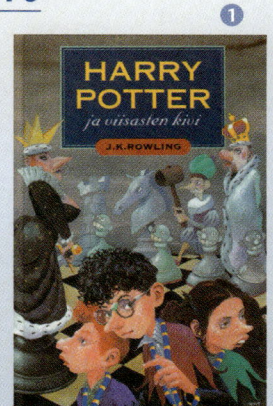

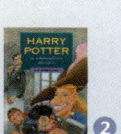

	Price Paid	Value
Book 1	$	$
Book 2	$	$
Book 3*	$	$

10

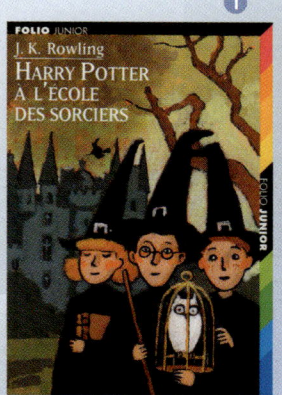

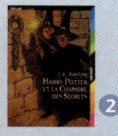

Finnish

	Price Paid	Value
Book 1	$	$
Book 2	$	$
Book 3	$	$

11

French

	Price Paid	Value
Book 1	$	$
Book 2	$	$
Book 3	$	$

Page Totals: | Price Paid | Total Value

COLLECTOR'S VALUE GUIDE™

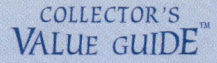

International Books

Value Guide – Harry Potter

International Books

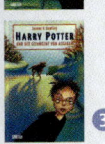

12

German

	Price Paid	Value
Book 1	$	$
Book 2	$	$
Book 3	$	$

13

Greek

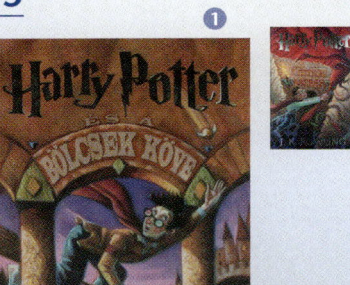

Photo Unavailable

	Price Paid	Value
Book 1*	$	$
Book 2*	$	$
Book 3*	$	$

14

Hebrew

	Price Paid	Value
Book 1	$	$
Book 2	$	$

15

Hungarian

	Price Paid	Value
Book 1	$	$
Book 2	$	$

Page Totals: Price Paid | Total Value

COLLECTOR'S VALUE GUIDE™

Value Guide – Harry Potter

16

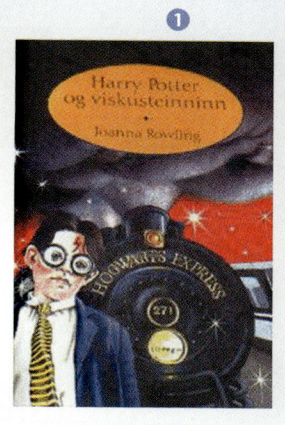

Icelandic

	Price Paid	Value
Book 1	$	$
Book 2*	$	$

17

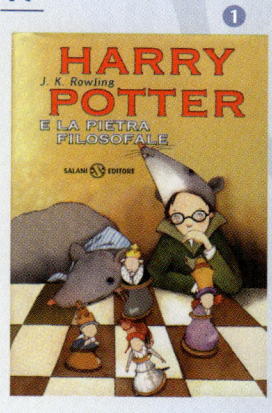

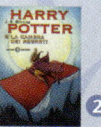

Italian

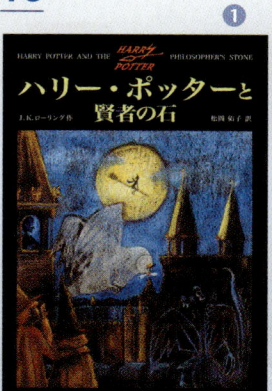

	Price Paid	Value
Book 1	$	$
Book 2	$	$
Book 3	$	$

18

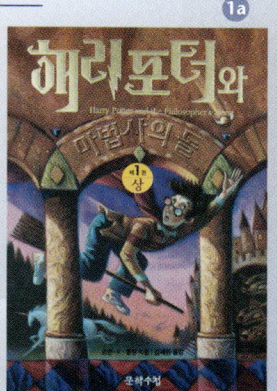

Japanese

	Price Paid	Value
Book 1	$	$
Book 2	$	$

19

Korean

	Price Paid	Value
Book 1a	$	$
Book 1b	$	$
Book 2a	$	$
Book 2b	$	$

International Books

COLLECTOR'S VALUE GUIDE™

Page Totals: Price Paid | Total Value

Value Guide – Harry Potter

International Books

19

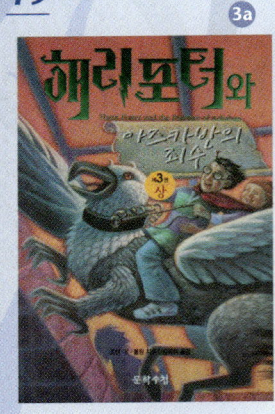

Korean, cont.

	Price Paid	Value
Book 3a	$	$
Book 3b	$	$

Each Korean book is available in 2 parts, sold separately.

20

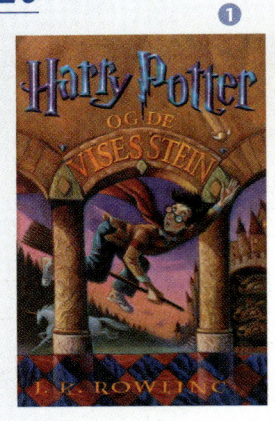

Norwegian

	Price Paid	Value
Book 1	$	$
Book 2	$	$

21

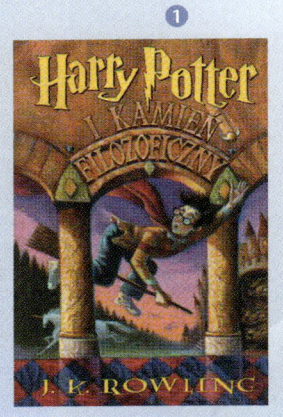

Polish

	Price Paid	Value
Book 1	$	$
Book 2*	$	$

22

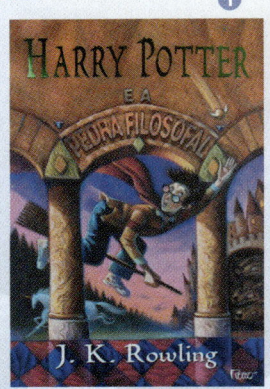

Portuguese (Brazil)

	Price Paid	Value
Book 1	$	$
Book 2	$	$

Page Totals: Price Paid | Total Value

COLLECTOR'S VALUE GUIDE

Value Guide – Harry Potter

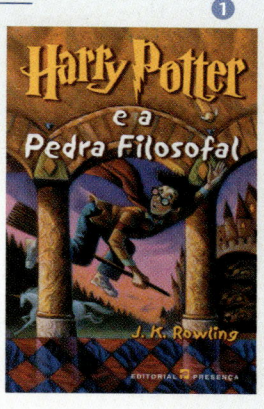

23

Portuguese (Portugal)

	Price Paid	Value
Book 1	$	$
Book 2	$	$
Book 3	$	$

24

Coming Soon

Romanian

	Price Paid	Value

25

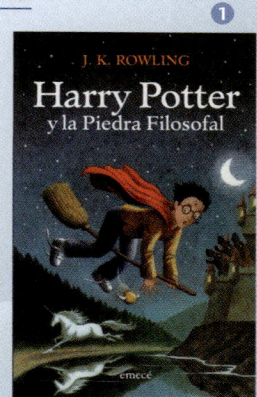

Photo Unavailable

Slovenian

	Price Paid	Value
Book 1*	$	$

26

Spanish (Castilian)

	Price Paid	Value
Book 1	$	$
Book 2	$	$
Book 3	$	$

Page Totals: Price Paid | Total Value

International Books

COLLECTOR'S VALUE GUIDE™

Value Guide – Harry Potter

27

Photo Unavailable

Spanish (Catalonian)

	Price Paid	Value
Book 1*	$	$
Book 2*	$	$

28

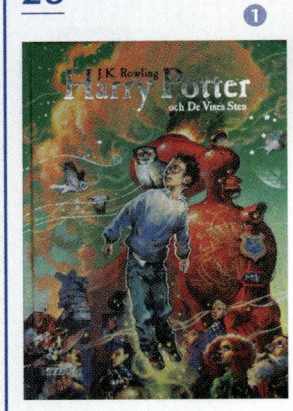

Swedish

	Price Paid	Value
Book 1	$	$
Book 2	$	$

29

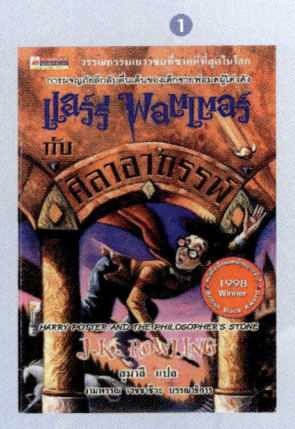

Thai

	Price Paid	Value
Book 1	$	$
Book 2*	$	$

30

Photo Unavailable

Turkish

	Price Paid	Value
Book 1*	$	$

Page Totals: Price Paid / Total Value

COLLECTOR'S VALUE GUIDE™

Collectibles Showcase

Department 56®

Seven Harry Potter-themed pieces will be included in Department 56's new *Hot Properties!* line for 2000. Six Secret Boxes™ will be available and limited to 2000 production – all of which come with a charm attached and hidden surprises inside.

1

Harry Potter™
Secret Box™
Item #: 59008 • Issued: 2000

Retail	Price Paid	Value
$19.50-22	$	$

2

Artist Rendering, Not Actual Product

Harry Potter™
Animated Scene
Animated Scene
Item #: 59006 • Issued: 2000

Retail	Price Paid	Value
N/A	$	$

3

Harry Potter™
The Golden Snitch™
Secret Box™
Item #: 59007 • Issued: 2000

Retail	Price Paid	Value
$12.50-14	$	$

COLLECTOR'S VALUE GUIDE™

Page Totals:	Price Paid	Total Value

Department 56®

Collectibles Showcase

4

Harry Potter™ Harry And Hagrid™ At Gringotts™
Secret Box™
Item #: 59012 • Issued: 2000

Retail	Price Paid	Value
$27.50-30	$	$

5

Harry Potter™ Harry And The Sorting Hat™
Secret Box™
Item #: 59010 • Issued: 2000

Retail	Price Paid	Value
$19.50-22	$	$

6

Hedwig™ The Owl
Secret Box™
Item #: 59009 • Issued: 2000

Retail	Price Paid	Value
$19.50-22	$	$

7

Hermione™ The Bookworm
Secret Box™
Item #: 59011 • Issued: 2000

Retail	Price Paid	Value
$19.50-22	$	$

Page Totals:	Price Paid	Total Value

COLLECTOR'S VALUE GUIDE™

Collectibles Showcase

Enesco

Among the Harry Potter products that Enesco plans to release in 2000 are four Storyteller Figurines, two Bookend Buddies and a wide variety of Story Scopes and Collector Stones. Story Scopes feature a viewer, that when looked into, reveals a secret tale. Collector Stones come in all different shapes, sizes and colors, including a rare Golden Snitch.

1

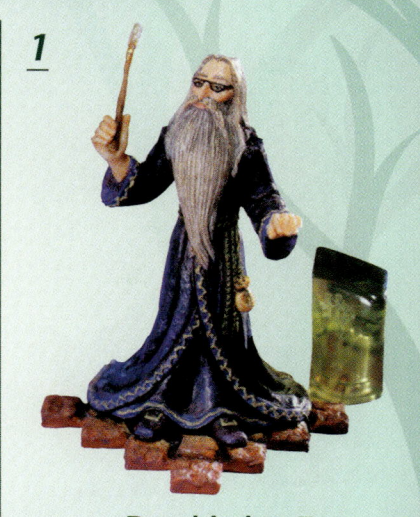

Dumbledore™
Mini Figurine With Story Scope
Item #: 811866 • Issued: 2000

Retail	Price Paid	Value
$12⁵⁰-14	$	$

2

Fluffy
Storyteller Figurine
Item #: 823235 • Issued: 2000

Retail	Price Paid	Value
$20-22	$	$

3

Hagrid™
Mini Figurine With Story Scope
Item #: 811874 • Issued: 2000

Retail	Price Paid	Value
$12⁵⁰-14	$	$

Page Totals:	Price Paid	Total Value

Collectibles Showcase

4

Harry
Large Character Bookend Buddy
Item #: 836265 • Issued: 2000

Retail	Price Paid	Value
$22⁵⁰-25	$	$

5

Harry
Mini Figurine With Story Scope
Item #: 811831 • Issued: 2000

Retail	Price Paid	Value
$12⁵⁰-14	$	$

6

Harry Potter Collector Stones
Collector Stones (25 designs, each sold separately)
Item #: 847852 • Issued: 2000

Retail	Price Paid	Value
$4⁹⁹-6 each	$	$

Page Totals: Price Paid | Total Value

COLLECTOR'S VALUE GUIDE™

Collectibles Showcase

Enesco

7

Harry
Storyteller Figurine
Item #: 823600 • Issued: 2000

Retail	Price Paid	Value
$20-22	$	$

8

Hedwig™
Mini Figurine With Story Scope
Item #: 811904 • Issued: 2000

Retail	Price Paid	Value
$12^{50}-14	$	$

9

Hermione
Large Character Bookend Buddy
Item #: 843113 • Issued: 2000

Retail	Price Paid	Value
$22^{50}-25	$	$

10

Hermione
Mini Figurine With Story Scope
Item #: 811858 • Issued: 2000

Retail	Price Paid	Value
$12^{50}-14	$	$

COLLECTOR'S VALUE GUIDE™

Page Totals:	Price Paid	Total Value

Collectibles Showcase

11

Hermione
Storyteller Figurine
Item #: 823619 • Issued: 2000

Retail	Price Paid	Value
$20-22	$	$

12

Ron
Mini Figurine With Story Scope
Item #: 811947 • Issued: 2000

Retail	Price Paid	Value
$12^{50}-14	$	$

13

Ron
Storyteller Figurine
Item #: 823627 • Issued: 2000

Retail	Price Paid	Value
$20-22	$	$

Enesco

Page Totals: Price Paid / Total Value

COLLECTOR'S VALUE GUIDE™

Collectibles Showcase

14

Story Scopes
Story Scopes (12 designs, each sold separately)
Item #: 844853 • Issued: 2000

Retail	Price Paid	Value
$4-5 each	$	$

15

Sorting Hat & Book Stack Bookends
Bookends
Item #: 823260 • Issued: 2000

Retail	Price Paid	Value
$30-33	$	$

16

Through The Trapdoor
Masterpiece Collector Figurine
Item #: 823597 • Issued: 2000

Retail	Price Paid	Value
$40-45	$	$

Enesco

COLLECTOR'S VALUE GUIDE™

Page Totals:	Price Paid	Total Value

Collectibles Showcase

Kurt S. Adler

Hogwarts students may want to stay away from the Whomping Willow, but collectors will want to decorate their holiday trees with 26 festive Harry Potter-themed decorations from Kurt S. Adler. The collection includes a holiday stocking, a glass ball, a set of lights and 23 tin, resin and Polonaise ornaments.

1

Bertie Bott's Beans
Tin Ornament
Item #: HP103 • Issued: 2000

Retail	Price Paid	Value
$9-10	$	$

2

Flying Keys
Tin Ornament
Item #: HP103 • Issued: 2000

Retail	Price Paid	Value
$9-10	$	$

3

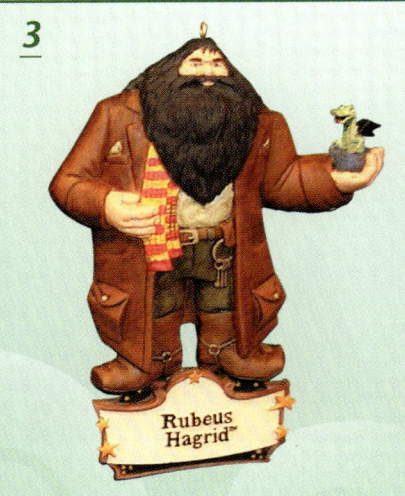

Hagrid With Norbert
Bas Relief Resin Ornament
Item #: HP100 • Issued: 2000

Retail	Price Paid	Value
$8-10	$	$

Page Totals:	Price Paid	Total Value

COLLECTOR'S VALUE GUIDE™

Collectibles Showcase

4
Harry And Hedwig
Polonaise Ornament
Item #: AP1266 • Issued: 2000

Retail	Price Paid	Value
$50-55	$	$

5
back view

Harry, Hermione And Ron Chasing Keys
Printed Glass Ball Ornament
Item #: HP104 • Issued: 2000

Retail	Price Paid	Value
$8-10	$	$

6
Harry Holding Cauldron And Potions
Full Round Resin Ornament
Item #: HP102 • Issued: 2000

Retail	Price Paid	Value
$10-12	$	$

7
Harry On Nimbus 2000
Blow Mold Ornament
Item #: HP105 • Issued: 2000

Retail	Price Paid	Value
$4-5	$	$

Kurt S. Adler

COLLECTOR'S VALUE GUIDE™

Page Totals:	Price Paid	Total Value

Collectibles Showcase

Kurt S. Adler

8

Harry Playing Quidditch
Light Set
Item #: HP107 • Issued: 2000

Retail	Price Paid	Value
$22⁵⁰-25	$	$

9

Artist Rendering, Not Actual Product

Harry Playing Quidditch
Polonaise Ornament
Item #: AP1263 • Issued: 2000

Retail	Price Paid	Value
$50-55	$	$

10

Photo Unavailable

Harry With Gifts Christmas Morning
Blow Mold Ornament
Item #: HP105 • Issued: 2000

Retail	Price Paid	Value
$4-5	$	$

11

Harry With Wand And Hedwig
Bas Relief Resin Ornament
Item #: HP100 • Issued: 2000

Retail	Price Paid	Value
$8-10	$	$

Page Totals: Price Paid _____ Total Value _____

COLLECTOR'S VALUE GUIDE™

Collectibles Showcase

Kurt S. Adler

12
Harry With Wand Lighting Tree
Applique Stocking
Item #: HP108 • Issued: 2000

Retail	Price Paid	Value
$22.50-25	$	$

13
Hat Icon
Full Round Resin Ornament
Item #: HP101 • Issued: 2000

Retail	Price Paid	Value
$5.50-6	$	$

14
Hedwig With Letter
Full Round Resin Ornament
Item #: HP109 • Issued: 2000

Retail	Price Paid	Value
$10-12	$	$

15
Artist Rendering, Not Actual Product

Hermione Mixing Potions
Full Round Resin Ornament
Item #: HP102 • Issued: 2000

Retail	Price Paid	Value
$10-12	$	$

Page Totals: Price Paid / Total Value

COLLECTOR'S VALUE GUIDE™

Kurt S. Adler

Collectibles Showcase

16
Hermione With Book Of Scales
Polonaise Ornament
Item #: AP1265 • Issued: 2000

Retail	Price Paid	Value
$50-55	$	$

17
Hermione With Wand & Feathers
Bas Relief Resin Ornament
Item #: HP100 • Issued: 2000

Retail	Price Paid	Value
$8-10	$	$

18
Key Icon
Full Round Resin Ornament
Item #: HP101 • Issued: 2000

Retail	Price Paid	Value
$5^{50}-6	$	$

19
Lightning Bolt (set/3)
Injection Plastic
Item #: HP106 • Issued: 2000

Retail	Price Paid	Value
$5^{50}-6	$	$

Page Totals: Price Paid / Total Value

COLLECTOR'S VALUE GUIDE™

Collectibles Showcase

20
Mirror Icon
Full Round Resin Ornament
Item #: HP101 • Issued: 2000

Retail	Price Paid	Value
$5^{50}-6	$	$

21
Nimbus
Tin Ornament
Item #: HP103 • Issued: 2000

Retail	Price Paid	Value
$9-10	$	$

22
Nimbus Icon
Full Round Resin Ornament
Item #: HP101 • Issued: 2000

Retail	Price Paid	Value
$5^{50}-6	$	$

23
Norbert With Egg
Full Round Resin Ornament
Item #: HP109 • Issued: 2000

Retail	Price Paid	Value
$10-12	$	$

Kurt S. Adler

COLLECTOR'S VALUE GUIDE™

Page Totals: | Price Paid | Total Value |

Collectibles Showcase

24

Ron In Sorting Hat
Full Round Resin Ornament
Item #: HP102 • Issued: 2000

Retail	Price Paid	Value
$10-12	$	$

25

Ron With Scabbers
Polonaise Ornament
Item #: AP1264 • Issued: 2000

Retail	Price Paid	Value
$50-55	$	$

26

Ron With Wand & Flopped Experiment
Bas Relief Resin Ornament
Item #: HP100 • Issued: 2000

Retail	Price Paid	Value
$8-10	$	$

Page Totals: Price Paid ___ Total Value ___

COLLECTOR'S VALUE GUIDE™

Kurt S. Adler

Collectibles Showcase

Hallmark

Hallmark will be releasing many new collectibles based on Harry Potter's magical world. With items ranging from water globes and Keepsake Ornaments to key chains and pens, there is something for everyone. In addition, there will be plenty of other Hallmark merchandise from home decor to party supplies.

1

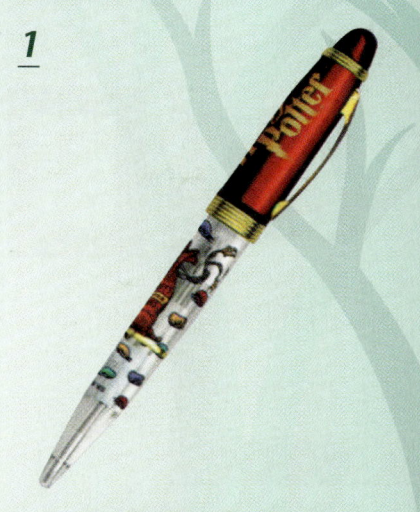

Bertie Bott's™ Beans
Light-Up Pen
Item #: 995HRP7356 • Issued: 2000

Retail	Price Paid	Value
$9⁹⁵	$	$

2

Chess Game
Water Globe
Item #: 1HAR2703 • Issued: 2000

Retail	Price Paid	Value
$7⁹⁵	$	$

3

Crests
Light-Up Pen
Item #: 995HRP7354 • Issued: 2000

Retail	Price Paid	Value
$9⁹⁵	$	$

Page Totals: | Price Paid | Total Value |

COLLECTOR'S VALUE GUIDE™

Collectibles Showcase

Hallmark

4
Frame changes appearance depending on viewing angle

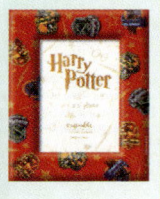

Crests/Sorting Hat™
Lenticular Padded Frame
Item #: 895HRP7300 • Issued: 2000

Retail	Price Paid	Value
$8.95	$	$

5

Devil's Snare
Water Globe
Item #: 1HAR2701 • Issued: 2000

Retail	Price Paid	Value
$7.95	$	$

6
Artist Rendering, Not Actual Product

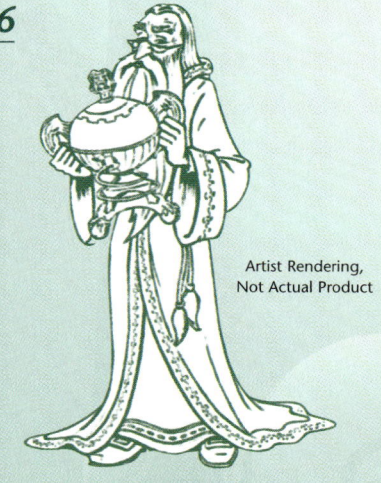

Dumbledore™ Figure
Figurine
Item #: 1895SFF3124 • Issued: 2000

Retail	Price Paid	Value
$18.95	$	$

7

Fat Lady Bookends (set/2)
Bookends (books not included)
Item #: 1HAR2717 • Issued: 2000

Retail	Price Paid	Value
$44.95	$	$

Page Totals: | Price Paid | Total Value |

COLLECTOR'S VALUE GUIDE™

Collectibles Showcase

8

Fluffy™ Door Stop
Door Stop
Item #: 1HAR2709 • Issued: 2000

Retail	Price Paid	Value
$34.95	$	$

9

Artist Rendering, Not Actual Product

Fluffy™ on Trinket Box
Trinket Box
Item #: 1495SFF3134 • Issued: 2000

Retail	Price Paid	Value
$14.95	$	$

10

Golden Snitch™ Key Chain
Key Chain
Item #: 1HAR2727 • Issued: 2000

Retail	Price Paid	Value
$5.95	$	$

11

Artist Rendering, Not Actual Product

Golden Snitch™ Lamp
Lamp
Item #: 1HAR2720 • Issued: 2000

Retail	Price Paid	Value
$39.95	$	$

Hallmark

COLLECTOR'S VALUE GUIDE™

Page Totals:	Price Paid	Total Value

Collectibles Showcase

Hallmark

12
Gringott's™ Bank
Bank
Item #: 1HAR2710 • Issued: 2000

Retail	Price Paid	Value
$24⁹⁵	$	$

13
Hagrid™ Door Decoration
Door Decoration
Item #: 1HAR2721 • Issued: 2000

Retail	Price Paid	Value
$14⁹⁵	$	$

14
Artist Rendering, Not Actual Product

Hagrid™ Figure
Figurine
Item #: 2495SFF3131 • Issued: 2000

Retail	Price Paid	Value
$24⁹⁵	$	$

15
Harry Potter™
Keepsake Ornament
Item #: 1295QXE4381 • Issued: 2000

Retail	Price Paid	Value
$12⁹⁵	$	$

Page Totals: Price Paid ___ Total Value ___

COLLECTOR'S VALUE GUIDE™

Collectibles Showcase

16

Harry Potter And The Sorcerer's Stone Numbered Edition Lunch Box
Lunch Box
Item #: 1095QXE8831 • Issued: 2000

Retail	Price Paid	Value
$10⁹⁵	$	$

17

Harry Potter™ Logo Key Chain
Key Chain
Item #: 1HAR2726 • Issued: 2000

Retail	Price Paid	Value
$4⁹⁵	$	$

18

Hedwig™
Light-Up Pen
Item #: 995HRP7352 • Issued: 2000

Retail	Price Paid	Value
$9⁹⁵	$	$

19

Hedwig the Owl™
Keepsake Ornament
Item #: 795QXE4394 • Issued: 2000

Retail	Price Paid	Value
$7⁹⁵	$	$

Hallmark

COLLECTOR'S VALUE GUIDE™

Page Totals: | Price Paid | Total Value |

Collectibles Showcase

20

Hedwig the Owl™ Scroll Room Decor
Scroll Room Decor
Item #: 1295SFF3121 • Issued: 2000

Retail	Price Paid	Value
$12.95	$	$

21

Hermione Granger™
Keepsake Ornament
Item #: 1295QXE4391 • Issued: 2000

Retail	Price Paid	Value
$12.95	$	$

22

Artist Rendering, Not Actual Product

Hermione Granger™ Holding Book Figure
Figurine
Item #: 1895SFF311 • Issued: 2000

Retail	Price Paid	Value
$18.95	$	$

23

Hogwarts™ Charms (set of 6)
Keepsake Ornaments
Item #: 1295QXE4404 • Issued: 2000

Retail	Price Paid	Value
$12.95	$	$

Page Totals:	Price Paid	Total Value

COLLECTOR'S VALUE GUIDE™

Collectibles Showcase

24
Hogwarts™ Crest
Light-Up Pen
Item #: 995HRP7355 • Issued: 2000

Retail	Price Paid	Value
$9.95	$	$

25
Hogwarts™ Emblem Ceramic Mug
Mug
Item #: 1HAR2725 • Issued: 2000

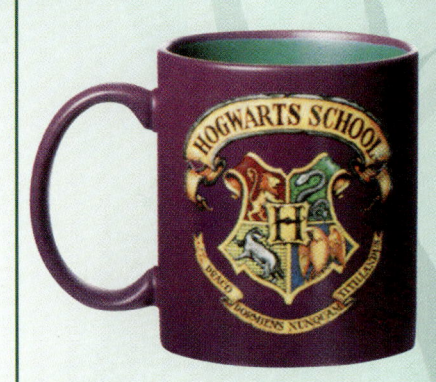

Retail	Price Paid	Value
$9.95	$	$

26
Lightning Bolts
Light-Up Pen
Item #: 995HRP7350 • Issued: 2000

Retail	Price Paid	Value
$9.95	$	$

27
Frame changes appearance depending on viewing angle

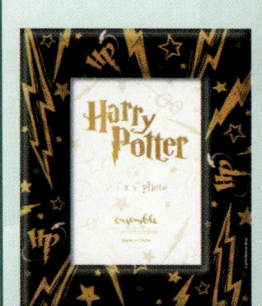

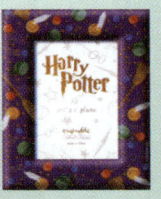

Lightning Bolts/ Quidditch™ Pattern
Lenticular Padded Frame
Item #: 895HRP7275 • Issued: 2000

Retail	Price Paid	Value
$8.95	$	$

Hallmark

COLLECTOR'S VALUE GUIDE™

Page Totals:	Price Paid	Total Value

Collectibles Showcase

28
Mirror of Erised™
Water Globe
Item #: 1HAR2705 • Issued: 2000

Retail	Price Paid	Value
$7⁹⁵	$	$

29
Norbert™
Light-Up Pen
Item #: 995HRP7353 • Issued: 2000

Retail	Price Paid	Value
$9⁹⁵	$	$

30
Artist Rendering, Not Actual Product

Norbert the Dragon™ Figure
Figurine
Item #: 1495SFF3114 • Issued: 2000

Retail	Price Paid	Value
$14⁹⁵	$	$

31
Potion Bottle Pen/Paper Gift Set
Pen & Paper Gift Set
Item #: 1HAR2706 • Issued: 2000

Retail	Price Paid	Value
$29⁹⁵	$	$

Page Totals: Price Paid | Total Value

Collectibles Showcase

32
Potion, Chess and Key
Light-Up Pen
Item #: 995HRP7357 • Issued: 2000

Retail	Price Paid	Value
$9⁹⁵	$	$

33
Potions Riddle
Water Globe
Item #: 1HAR2704 • Issued: 2000

Retail	Price Paid	Value
$7⁹⁵	$	$

34
Professor Dumbledore™
Keepsake Ornament
Item #: 1295QXE4384 • Issued: 2000

Retail	Price Paid	Value
$12⁹⁵	$	$

35
Quidditch™ Balls
Light-Up Pen
Item #: 995HRP7351 • Issued: 2000

Retail	Price Paid	Value
$9⁹⁵	$	$

COLLECTOR'S VALUE GUIDE™

Page Totals:	Price Paid	Total Value

Hallmark

Collectibles Showcase

36
Artist Rendering, Not Actual Product

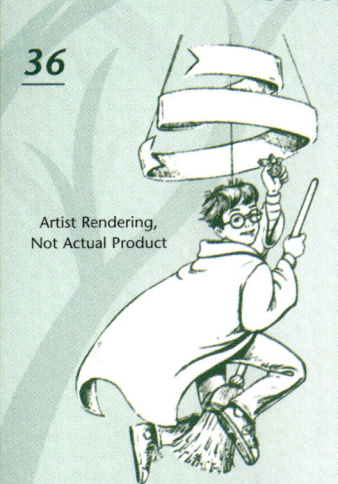

Quidditch Harry Potter™ Figure
Figurine
Item #: 1895SFF3101 • Issued: 2000

Retail	Price Paid	Value
$18⁹⁵	$	$

37

Quidditch™ Pen/ Paper Gift Set
Pen/Paper Gift Set
Item #: 1HAR2707 • Issued: 2000

Retail	Price Paid	Value
$29⁹⁵	$	$

38
Artist Rendering, Not Actual Product

Ron Weasley™ Figure
Figurine
Item #: 1895SFF3104 • Issued: 2000

Retail	Price Paid	Value
$18⁹⁵	$	$

39

Three-headed Dog
Water Globe
Item #: 1HAR2700 • Issued: 2000

Retail	Price Paid	Value
$7⁹⁵	$	$

Page Totals: Price Paid | Total Value

Collectibles Showcase

40

Winged Keys
Water Globe
Item #: 1HAR2702 • Issued: 2000

Retail	Price Paid	Value
$7⁹⁵	$	$

Hallmark

COLLECTOR'S
VALUE GUIDE™

Page Totals: | Price Paid | Total Value

143

Harry Potter Product Diary

This diary section is designed for you to record future Harry Potter releases from the officially licensed manufacturers. Exciting new Harry Potter products are being released almost daily, but you won't need a crystal ball to keep up with them. Just stay tuned to *www.CollectorsQuest.com* for regular updates on Harry Potter new releases and then fill in the information on the following pages.

The first page of this section can be filled with future release information from each of the manufacturers included in the *Collectibles Showcase* section on pages 119-143. The rest of the section is organized by product category in the following order: toys & games, apparel, school supplies, home decor and party supplies. Each manufacturer is listed in alphabetical order within their appropriate section. Enjoy your search for more Harry Potter products!

Collectibles Showcase
Department 56®

	Date Purch.	Price Paid	How Many	Total Value

Enesco

Hallmark

Kurt S. Adler

COLLECTOR'S VALUE GUIDE™

Page Totals: Price Paid ____ Total Value ____

Harry Potter Product Diary

Toys & Games

	Date Purch.	Price Paid	How Many	Total Value
Bachmann Trains				
Electronic Arts				
Fisher-Price®				
Flying Colors				

Page Totals: Price Paid | Total Value

COLLECTOR'S VALUE GUIDE™

Toys & Games
LEGO®

Mattel

Tiger Electronics®

Date Purch.	Price Paid	How Many	Total Value

Page Totals: Price Paid / Total Value

Toys & Games

	Date Purch.	Price Paid	How Many	Total Value
Schylling				
Toy Biz				
University Games				
Wizards of the Coast				

Page Totals: Price Paid _____ Total Value _____

Apparel

	Date Purch.	Price Paid	How Many	Total Value
Accessory Network				
Adorable Kids Inc.				
Berkshire Rainwear				

Page Totals:	Price Paid	Total Value

Apparel
Briefly Stated

	Date Purch.	Price Paid	How Many	Total Value

Changes

Fossil

Page Totals: Price Paid | Total Value

Apparel
Giant Merchandising

Date Purch.	Price Paid	How Many	Total Value

Happy Kids

Date Purch.	Price Paid	How Many	Total Value

High Point

Date Purch.	Price Paid	How Many	Total Value

Isaac Morris

Date Purch.	Price Paid	How Many	Total Value

Harry Potter Product Diary

COLLECTOR'S VALUE GUIDE™

Page Totals: | Price Paid | Total Value |

Apparel

Jaclyn

Jerry Leigh

Monterey Canyon

	Date Purch.	Price Paid	How Many	Total Value

Page Totals: Price Paid / Total Value

COLLECTOR'S VALUE GUIDE™

Apparel

Multiprint Manufacturing

	Date Purch.	Price Paid	How Many	Total Value

Novel Teez Designs

Pan Oceanic Eyewear

Page Totals: Price Paid ___ Total Value ___

Harry Potter Product Diary

COLLECTOR'S VALUE GUIDE™

Harry Potter Product Diary

Apparel
Sara Max

	Date Purch.	Price Paid	How Many	Total Value

Totes Isotoner

	Date Purch.	Price Paid	How Many	Total Value

Tri-Star Merchandise/Starline Creations

	Date Purch.	Price Paid	How Many	Total Value

Page Totals: Price Paid _____ Total Value _____

COLLECTOR'S VALUE GUIDE

School Supplies

All Night Media

Andrews McMeel

Cedco Publishing

Johnson & Johnson

Thermos®

Date Purch.	Price Paid	How Many	Total Value

Harry Potter Product Diary

COLLECTOR'S VALUE GUIDE™

Page Totals: | Price Paid | Total Value

155

Home Decor

	Date Purch.	Price Paid	How Many	Total Value
Madame Alexander				
Crown Crafts				
Encore/Xpres®				

Page Totals: Price Paid ____ Total Value ____

Home Decor
Fetco International

Date Purch.	Price Paid	How Many	Total Value

Franco Manufacturing

Gund®

Page Totals: Price Paid / Total Value

Harry Potter Product Diary
Collector's Value Guide

Harry Potter Product Diary

Home Decor

P.J. Kids®

	Date Purch.	Price Paid	How Many	Total Value

Springs Industries

TerriSol

Page Totals: Price Paid _____ Total Value _____

COLLECTOR'S VALUE GUIDE™

Party Supplies
DecoPac

	Date Purch.	Price Paid	How Many	Total Value

Elope

M & D Industries

Page Totals: Price Paid _____ Total Value _____

Harry Potter Product Diary

Party Supplies

OddzOn

	Date Purch.	Price Paid	How Many	Total Value

Rubie's Costumes

Wilton Industries

Remember to check our web site, www.CollectorsQuest.com, for news of future Harry Potter product releases!

Page Totals: Price Paid | Total Value

COLLECTOR'S VALUE GUIDE™

Total Value Of My Collection

Record your collection here by adding the totals from the bottom of each page.

Harry Potter Books

Page Number	Price Paid	Total Value
Page 105		
Page 106		
Page 107		
Page 108		
Page 109		
Page 110		
Page 111		
Page 112		
Page 113		
Page 114		
Page 115		
Page 116		
Page 117		
Page 118		

Department 56®

Page Number	Price Paid	Total Value
Page 119		
Page 120		
Subtotal:		

Enesco

Page Number	Price Paid	Total Value
Page 121		
Page 122		
Page 123		
Page 124		
Page 125		

Kurt S. Adler

Page Number	Price Paid	Total Value
Page 126		
Page 127		
Page 128		
Page 129		
Page 130		
Page 131		
Page 132		

Hallmark

Page Number	Price Paid	Total Value
Page 133		
Page 134		
Page 135		
Subtotal:		

COLLECTOR'S VALUE GUIDE™

Page Totals:	Price Paid	Total Value

Total Value Of My Collection

Record your collection here by adding the totals from the bottom of each page.

Hallmark, cont.

Page Number	Price Paid	Total Value
Page 136		
Page 137		
Page 138		
Page 139		
Page 140		
Page 141		
Page 142		
Page 143		

Harry Potter Product Diary

Page Number	Price Paid	Total Value
Page 144		
Page 145		
Page 146		
Page 147		
Page 148		
Page 149		
Page 150		
Page 151		
Subtotal:		

Harry Potter Product Diary

Page Number	Price Paid	Total Value
Page 152		
Page 153		
Page 154		
Page 155		
Page 156		
Page 157		
Page 158		
Page 159		
Page 160		
Subtotal:		

Page Totals:	Price Paid	Total Value

COLLECTOR'S VALUE GUIDE™

A Wizard's Guide To The Secondary Market

Harry Potter merchandise will soon be popping up everywhere, from department stores to mass market chains. But what happens when the collectible you want is no longer available in retail stores? Well, hop on your broomsticks as we transport ourselves to the next best thing to the magical marketplace at Diagon Alley – the secondary market.

Desperately Seeking Harry

The best place to look for Harry Potter collectibles once they hit the secondary market will be through a piece of magic found in your own home – the Internet. On-line stores are sure to have plenty of merchandise available and many will specialize in Harry Potter items. Mailing lists, chat rooms and bulletin boards (such as ours at www.CollectorsQuest.com) are a good way to touch base with other collectors who may be looking to buy or sell merchandise. Another option is on-line auctions, where you can search and bid for specific items.

You may also scan the classified ads in your own local newspaper – someone may have exactly what you are looking for. The newspaper is especially helpful in announcing special events where Harry Potter merchandise may be available. (When searching for first edition or foreign Harry Potter books, you can use the phone book to locate used bookstores.)

PREDICTING THE MARKET

When it comes to book collecting, the first printing of the first edition is almost always the most collectible version. You should also be aware that first printings may have "points" or "states." These refer to changes or corrections made during the print run. The first issue is often the most valuable, followed closely and sometimes superseded by uncorrected proofs or advance reading copies. "Uncorrected proofs" refer to the earliest version of the book which has not yet been edited. Advance reading copies have typically been edited and are given out to reviewers and booksellers.

An Enesco Story Scope which was given away at a trade show during a Harry Potter promotion.

It is important to familiarize yourself with the terminology that booksellers use. When most sellers say first edition, they usually mean the first printing of the first edition – that is, the first books to actually leave the printers and be shipped to stores. But beware. The Harry Potter books are all still in their first edition, so if you see a seller who lists the book as a first edition with no specific printing number, you may want to double-check before you make your purchase.

Unless you have a crystal ball and some experience in divination, it is almost impossible to predict exactly which collectibles will increase in value. However, there are several points to take into consideration. Limited edi-

> 24 23 22 21 20 19 18 17 16 15   9/9 0/0 1 2 3 4
> Printed in the U.S.A.   23
> First American edition, October 1999

A book's printing information can usually be found on the back of the title page. The numbers on the top left indicate the print run, while the numbers on the right indicate the date of publication. (This is the 15th printing of Book 3.)

tion and promotional items are sure to command a higher value on the secondary market. Many promotional items have been released at trade and gift shows by licensed manufacturers to showcase upcoming products. Also, several pieces are being released as Warner Bros. Studio Store exclusives.

Caring For Your Collection

Condition means everything to the value of your collection. Books should be stored out of direct sunlight, heat and humidity. The condition of a book is normally described using a grading system. But remember, grading is very subjective – what you consider a minor flaw may be a major flaw to someone else. Many hardcover books come with dust jackets, which are very easily creased or torn. A missing or damaged dust jacket can seriously reduce the value of a book. Many booksellers give hardcover books two grades, the first for the book and the second for the dust jacket.

Torn Harry Potter and the Sorcerer's Stone dust jacket.

When it comes to collectibles, to get full value, the piece should be in good-as-new condition. Even tiny flaws – such as chips, hairline cracks or faded paint – will detract from its value. To ensure your pieces' safety, store it in its packaging and keep it in an area that is low in heat and humidity. If you would like to display items like figurines, make sure to keep the original packaging and avoid sunlight to prevent fading.

A hairline crack, shown here on a Harry Potter frame from the Warner Bros. Studio Store, can affect secondary market value.

Map Of Great Britain

Use the corresponding map to follow author J. K. Rowling's adventures through Great Britain.

Near **Bristol** are the towns of Yates and Winterbourne, where J. K. Rowling spent part of her childhood.

Exeter is home to Exeter University, the school from which Rowling graduated.

Gloucester is home to the Gloucester Cathedral, which is reportedly the site of filming for the upcoming movie.

London is home to many important places in Harry Potter's world. Harry catches the magical Hogwarts Express at **King's Cross**, a London railroad station. Also, behind London's **Leaky Cauldron**, a pub for wizards, is **Diagon Alley**, where Hogwarts students shop for their back-to-school supplies.

On a delayed train commute from **Manchester** to London in 1990, Rowling came up with the concept of a story about a young boy attending a wizard school.

After Rowling's divorce, she moved to Edinburgh, to live with her sister, Di. Much of the first book was written by Rowling in **Edinburgh's** Nicholson's cafe.

Could Scotland be the site of the **Hogwarts School of Witchcraft and Wizardry**? Some experts think so, considering the number of hours that the students spend traveling north from London on the Hogwarts Express.

Map Of Great Britain

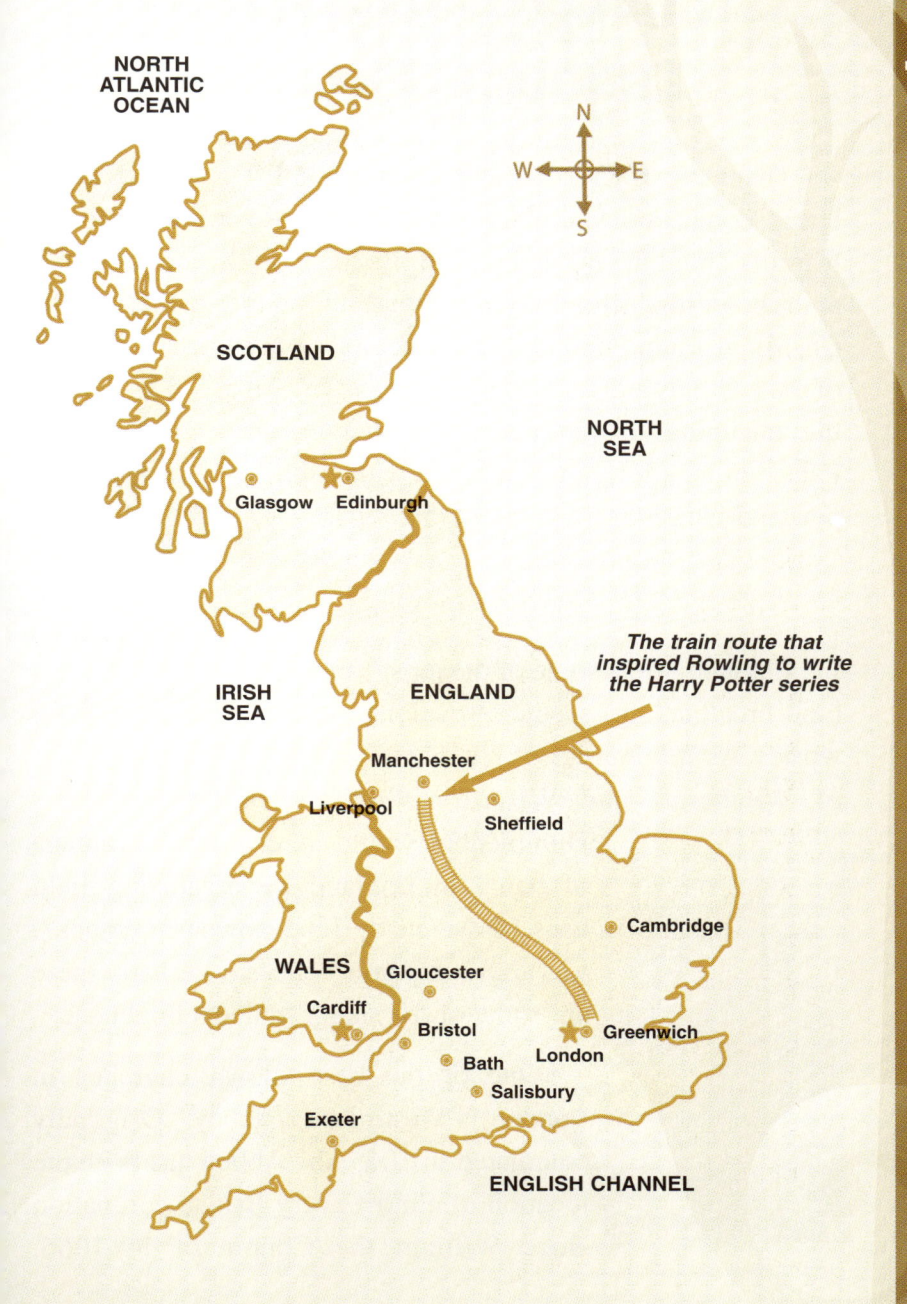

NORTH ATLANTIC OCEAN

N W E S

SCOTLAND

NORTH SEA

• Glasgow ★ Edinburgh

IRISH SEA

ENGLAND

The train route that inspired Rowling to write the Harry Potter series

• Manchester
• Liverpool
• Sheffield

• Cambridge

WALES
• Gloucester
★ Cardiff
• Bristol
• Bath
★ London • Greenwich
• Salisbury
• Exeter

ENGLISH CHANNEL

Journey With Harry Through England

Thanks to J. K. Rowling's phenomenally popular series of Harry Potter books, children and adults all over the world are learning about the ins and outs of life in Great Britain, from life at a boarding school to the ritual of adding coins to the Christmas Plum Pudding. Let's take a look at some of the customs and traditions that are as British as the changing of the guard at Buckingham Palace or an afternoon cup of tea with crumpets and jam.

A Tour Of England

England offers some of the most historic (and breathtaking) scenic attractions in the world. As headmaster of Hogwarts School of Witchcraft and Wizardry, Professor Dumbledore would surely take advantage of being in England by organizing field trips (powered by Floo powder, perhaps?) to various historic venues. Perhaps these are some of the sights students might see:

Professor Albus Dumbledore as depicted in a new Keepsake Ornament from Hallmark.

London's Westminster Abbey

One of the best known churches in London is Westminster Abbey. Originally completed in 1065, the Abbey has been the location of almost every British coronation since William the Conqueror in 1066.

Royal weddings and burials have also traditionally taken place in the church throughout the years. Following her tragic death, the funeral of Diana, Princess of Wales, took place at the famous abbey in September of 1997.

London's Buckingham Palace

To the west of London and on the banks of the River Thames lies the stately Windsor Castle which has been home to the Royal family for centuries. The London residence of reigning monarchs since 1837 has been Buckingham Palace. It is Buckingham Palace where visitors can see the traditionally garbed sentries guarding the entrance. The Palace serves as headquarters for Royal ceremonies, state visits and entertaining by the Royals.

The famous Crown Jewels are housed at The Tower of London which was built by William the Conqueror along the River Thames. Nearby is the Tower Bridge, another attraction for tourists, which connects North and South London. Among the other popular sites in London are Hyde Park, Number 10 Downing Street, which is the residence of the British Prime Minister, Trafalgar Square and the well-known Madame Tussaud's Wax Museum.

Changing Of The Guard

The change of the guards, which takes place at Buckingham Palace, occurs daily at precisely 11:30 a.m.

In southern England, a reminder of England's long history stands in the form of a circular megalithic structure which has come to be known as Stonehenge.

This prehistoric stone circle, which is believed to have been constructed about 4,000 years ago, has mystified historians through the ages. Just a short distance from Stonehenge, in the town of Bath, are hot mineral springs which have attracted visitors since the Roman conquerors during the first century A.D.

CELEBRATE YOUR HOLIDAYS IN HARRY POTTER STYLE

Halloween at the Hogwarts School's Great Hall is always a grand affair with flying bats and decorative lanterns made out of pumpkins. Halloween has its roots in ancient Britain, though nowadays it is more popular in the United States. The Celts and Druids celebrated "Samhain" – which means "summer's end" – at the end of each October. This, however, was not only a festival commemorating the end of the summer, but also a night when the spirits of the dead returned to visit the living. Bonfires were usually lit in order to prevent any bad spirits from staying and to encourage the good one spirits to linger.

To foster the festivities around Christmas, the students at Hogwarts rely upon a plethora of holiday favorites including Mince Pie and Christmas Plum Pudding which appear as if by magic, along with roast turkeys, peas, potatoes, gravy, cranberry sauce and chipolatas – a kind of meat sausage.

Christmas is also the traditional day to break open crackers – which are decorated paper tubes filled with a party hat, a gift and a joke. Christmas is followed by Boxing Day, which is observed on December 26 and is one of the many holidays that is observed at Hogwarts. The origins of this holiday have been attributed to several practices, including the medieval tradition of churches opening their poor boxes and distributing the alms and the distribution of gifts to servants or employees.

TIME TO GO
BACK TO SCHOOL!

The British educational system offers a choice of either state-run schools or privately-run "public" schools which charge a fee. In public schools, students may either attend classes daily and return home in the afternoon or they may live on campus throughout the school year.

Harry and his friends at Hogwarts are required to have a uniform consisting of a black robe, a pointed black hat and a black winter cloak. Uniforms are also required for both boys and girls in real British schools. These uniforms are usually blazers and trousers or a skirt. Although some boarding schools require outfits reflecting the school's colors, none would compare to the eye-catching outfit that is required at Smeltings – the school that Harry's cousin, Dudley, attends. The boys there are required to wear maroon "tailcoats," orange "knickerbockers" and straw hats which are referred to as "boaters."

Much like the students at Hogwarts, real English boarding school students live in dormitories called "houses." And also like at Hogwarts, each dormitory has an adult housemaster or mistress, a "head boy" or "head girl" and a "prefect," who is one of the oldest students in the house. Acting as the principal or superintendent of the school is the "headmaster," who oversees the operation of the entire school.

> ### The Testing Of A Prince
>
> Prince William, second in line after his father to inherit the throne of England, has reportedly scored well on his "A-levels." William is planning to attend the University of St. Andrews in Scotland. The prince is currently enjoying his "gap year," the year many British students take off before beginning college.

At around age of 16, students in England take the GCSE (General Certificate of Secondary Education), a series of qualifying examinations. During these last two years, students study for their A-levels, advanced exams which determine entry into a university. Similarly, the examinations Harry and his cohorts will be taking when they turn 15 are the "O.W.L.s" or the "Ordinary Wizarding Levels." The Higher level exams at Hogwarts are called the "N.E.W.T.s" – the "Nastily Exhausting Wizarding Tests."

ALL ABOARD!

Travel by rail is one of the most efficient, and popular, forms of transportation in England. Likewise, Harry finds it the perfect way to get to Hogwarts (when the Ford Angelina is unavailable). Other means of transportation include the distinctive red double-decker buses in London, which are regal but don't quite compare to the purple triple-decker bus known to Harry and his friends as the Knight Bus.

SICKLES AND SHILLINGS

The currency used in Harry Potter's wizarding world includes coinage known as the gold "Galleon," the silver "Sickle" and the bronze "Knut." According to Hagrid, one "Galleon" is worth 17 "Sickles" and one "Sickle" is worth 29 "Knuts." However, the monetary system in England is a little more complex as it includes several different coins including the fifty, twenty, ten, five and two pence. Prior to a conversion to the decimalizing of the currency system in 1971, coinage in Britain also included half crowns, shillings, guineas and half pennies.

"Wonga" In Your Pocket!

Some British slang and terms for money include words such as "dosh," "quid," "bob," "p," "wonga," "spondulicks," "fivers" and "tenners."

The English "Bobby"

The name for the English policeman, the "bobby," is from Sir Robert Peel (nicknamed "Bobby") who during the early 1800s, reorganized the British police force.

BONNETS AND BOOTS

All of the four Harry Potter titles released in the United States have had much of their vocabulary, "Americanized." Although English is spoken in both Great Britain and the United States, there are many differences between "British English" and "American English," including things like spelling, pronunciation, usage and slang. Abbreviations of crude sayings are popular among the British. For example, the word "blimey" is an expression of surprise and is derived from the phrase "God blind me!" Differences in terms for everyday items are noted when a person's nose is called a "conk" in Harry Potter's world. On a car in Britain, its hood is called its "bonnet" and its trunk compartment is its "boot."

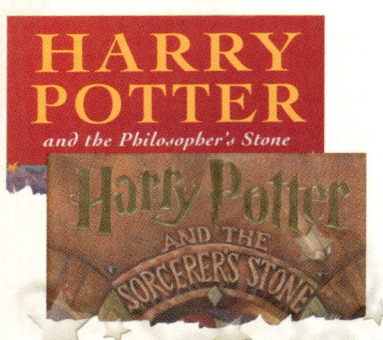

Although some differences in terminology still remain even after the text was changed for an American audience, Scholastic went through great pains to ensure that the published books would speak to children in the United States. For example, the title (as well as the cover) of the first book was changed from *Harry Potter and the Philosopher's Stone* to *Harry Potter and the Sorcerer's Stone*. Also, the word "jumper" was changed to sweater, "cinema" to movies, "sherbet lemon" to lemon drop, "holiday" to vacation and "dustbin" to trash can. It is also interesting to note that as the books are published throughout the world, several of the images and fonts have changed as well.

Harry Potter and the Philosopher's Stone, U.K. edition and *Harry Potter and the Sorcerer's Stone*, its American counterpart

SEEKERS AND KEEPERS

Popular English pastimes and recreational sports are similar to those found in America, only many have different names! British "football" is what Americans know as soccer, while the American version of football is called "American football" in

England. Many different British games are played on pocketed tables like pool and snooker. Snooker involves 15 red balls and six others of different colors with the intent being to "snooker" your opponent by blocking their opportunity for a direct shot. The British also enjoy playing cricket or participating in hurling – an Irish sport which is a cross between hockey and rugby.

Department 56's "Golden Snitch™" Secret Box™.

When Hagrid first tries to describe to Harry the game of Quidditch, the game played by wizards and witches, he compares it to soccer. Hagrid stumbles over the explanation of the rules, but Harry later gets a lesson from Oliver Wood, his Quidditch team captain. After Oliver explains the purpose of the balls – the Quaffle, Bludger and Golden Snitch – and the players – the Seeker, Keeper and Chasers – Harry remarks that Quidditch is similar to basketball, only played with flying broomsticks.

TREACLE TART AND A SPOT OF TEA

Dining in England is generally regarded as a basic diet of meat, potatoes, fish and vegetables. However, a meal's method of preparation and many of the foods' colorful names make the food distinctly British.

Bubble and Squeak . . .

The name "Bubble and Squeak" gets its name from the sound that mashed potatoes and cabbage make when they are fried in a skillet!

Like many of the British, Harry often enjoys a large breakfast, starting his days with a large assortment of foods such as: egg dishes, bacon, bangers (sausage), tomatoes and fried bread with bowls of porridge, pots of hot tea and crumpets served with marmalade or butter.

English pubs, such as The Hogshead, a real establishment in London, and the fictional The Three Broomsticks in Hogsmeade, provide authentic fare at a good value, along with a pint of beer (or butterbeer) or cider. Menus includes such favorites as bangers and mash (sausage links and mashed potatoes), bubble and squeak (a fried mashed potato and shredded cabbage patty) and jacket (baked) potatoes with Hot Treacle Pudding for "afters."

So even if you can't climb aboard the Hogwarts Express to journey to Harry's magical school, you can jump into a plane, train or automobile and a take a trip to Harry's homeland: a land called England.

What's Cooking In The Cauldron?!

Harry spent nearly 10 of his 11 years eating whatever was left after his cousin, Dudley, finished eating (which was often nothing!) and never had a birthday cake or even the smallest sweet treat. When he arrived at Hogwarts School of Witchcraft and Wizardry at the age of 11, Harry was greeted with the smells of wondrously sweet English puddings and tarts, filling steak and kidney pie, Yorkshire pudding, porridge and even Hagrid's specialties – rock cakes and treacle fudge. Here are some recipes for a few of the treats that has Harry enjoyed:

Rock Cakes

Rock cakes will become as "hard as rocks" if not eaten immediately after baking! Recipe makes about 3 dozen cookies.

> 3 eggs
> 1/4 cup milk
> 1 cup butter (softened)
> 3 cups flour
> 1 1/2 teaspoon baking powder
> 1 teaspoon salt
> 1/4 teaspoon nutmeg
> 3/4 cups sugar
> 1 cup dried currants

Preheat oven to 350 degrees.

Beat eggs with milk. Add softened butter and beat. Combine flour, baking powder, salt, nutmeg and sugar in separate bowl. Add flour mixture to egg, milk and butter mixture and mix until crumbly. Stir in currants. Drop spoonfuls of dough on greased cookie sheet about 2 inches apart. Bake until golden brown – about 15 minutes. Serve with tea.

Spotted Dog

This steamed pudding got its name from the raisins and currants that give it such a wonderful taste! A recipe for Custard Sauce is also included to help top it off.

1 cup flour
1 cup plus 4 tablespoons butter
1 cup breadcrumbs
3/4 cup raisins
3/4 cup currants
5 tablespoons sugar
pinch of salt
1/2 teaspoon pumpkin pie spice
1/2 cup plus 2 tablespoons milk

Mix all ingredients together except for the 4 tablespoons of butter. Use 2 tablespoons of butter to grease the inside of a large bowl and place dough in it. Melt the other 2 tablespoons of butter and brush top of dough. Brush a piece of foil with melted butter and loosely cover bowl, tie around rim with string. Place bowl on steamer rack or inverted saucer in large pot in about 3 inches of water. Steam for 2 1/2 hours, checking level of water and adding more, if necessary.

To serve, carefully remove the bowl from pot, remove the foil and run knife around the edge of bowl to loosen. Turn upside down onto serving platter and serve hot with Custard Sauce (see recipe below) or sprinkle with super-fine granulated sugar. Serves 4 to 6.

Custard Sauce:

> 1 1/2 cups milk
> 2 teaspoons cornstarch
> 1 tablespoon sugar
> 3 egg yolks
> 1/2 teaspoon vanilla extract

In heavy saucepan, combine 2 tablespoons of milk with cornstarch. When dissolved, add rest of milk and sugar and cook over medium heat until mixture boils and thickens. Place egg yolks in bowl and beat with fork. Slowly pour 1 cup of the hot sauce over egg yolks, beating constantly. Pour egg and sauce mixture into saucepan that contains the remainder of the sauce. Continue to stir until mixture returns to a boil. Add vanilla extract and remove from heat. Pour hot over Spotted Dog. Makes 2 cups.

Treacle Tart

Treacle Tart is a filled pie made of bread crumbs and treacle – which is a light golden molasses. Honey can be substituted for treacle.

> *pastry for one nine-inch pie*
> *2 cups treacle (molasses or honey)*
> *1 1/2 cups fresh white breadcrumbs*
> *1 teaspoon lemon juice*
> *finely grated peel of 1 lemon*
> *1 egg, beaten*
> *1 teaspoon water*

Preheat oven to 350 degrees.

Roll out pastry, line pie plate and crimp edges. Combine treacle, bread crumbs, lemon juice and grated lemon peel in bowl. Pour into pastry-lined pie plate.

Roll out remainder of pastry, cut into strips and arrange strips in lattice formation over the filling. Combine beaten egg with water and brush mixture over pastry top. Bake at 350 degrees for 10 minutes, then reduce heat to 300 degrees and continue baking for another 20 to 25 minutes, or until filling is set. Serve hot or cold, with whipped cream, if desired.

Trifle

Authentic Trifle is made with a layer of sherry and brandy-soaked cake, however, the alcohol may be omitted.

> 1 angel food or sponge cake
> 1 cup raspberry jam
> 1/4 cup slivered almonds
> 1/4 cup brandy
> 3/4 cup sherry
> 2 packages of vanilla custard or pudding mix
> 1 large container whipped cream
> sprig of fresh mint, candied fruit
>   or fresh strawberries for garnish

Cut cake into thick slices and spread each slice with raspberry jam. Arrange slices on bottom of large glass pedestal bowl. Sprinkle almonds over cake slices, pour on brandy and sherry (if desired).

Prepare pudding or custard according to package directions. Allow to set and then pour over cake. Let set, top with remaining raspberry jam and then cover with whipped cream. Decorate with candied fruit or strawberries. Refrigerate until ready to serve. Serves 6-8.

Fun Facts

When authors choose names for characters in their books, they often refer to foreign languages and word etymologies to convey personality traits and descriptions. It is evident that J. K. Rowling did just that in her research for Harry Potter.

Names

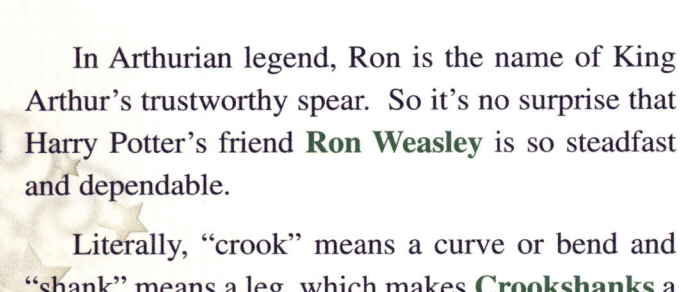

In Arthurian legend, Ron is the name of King Arthur's trustworthy spear. So it's no surprise that Harry Potter's friend **Ron Weasley** is so steadfast and dependable.

Literally, "crook" means a curve or bend and "shank" means a leg, which makes **Crookshanks** a very appropriate name for a bowlegged cat!

Kurt S. Adler ornament featuring Ron Weasley.

The bully at Hogwarts is named **Draco Malfoy** – an odd name, to be sure. But, considering the Latin and French meanings of the name, it certainly describes him perfectly. "Draco" is Latin for dragon, "mal" means bad or wrong in French and "foy" is derived from the Latin word meaning voyage or journey.

"Krumm" is a German word meaning curved or crooked – a perfect name for a boy described as having a "large curved nose" – which is how **Viktor Krum** is introduced in *Harry Potter and the Goblet of Fire*.

Artist's rendering of Hallmark's figurine featuring Norbert the dragon.

To describe the evil **Voldemort**, Rowling turned to two French words – "voler" meaning "to fly or to steal" and "mort" meaning "death."

Remus Lupin, one of the professors at the Hogwarts School, has a name based in Roman mythology. According to this mythology, Remus and his twin brother Romulus (the founder of Rome) were raised by a she-wolf and the word lupine means "wolflike."

In Greek mythology, "Argus" is a mythical watchman with a hundred eyes – which makes the name an appropriate one for **Argus Filch**, the Hogwarts School hall monitor.

The name of Filch's cat, **Mrs. Norris,** is also the name of a character in a novel written by Jane Austen, J. K. Rowling's favorite author. In *Mansfield Park*, Mrs. Norris is a hypocritical and nosy woman, similar to her Harry Potter counterpart, the cat who patrols the corridors of Hogwarts.

TRANSPORTATION

The **Nimbus Two Thousand** is the most coveted flying broom in Harry's world. A "nimbus" refers to a bright cloud that surrounds a god or goddess that appears on earth.

The **Hogwarts Express** is the name of the train that takes Hogwarts students directly to the school from Platform Nine and Three Quarters at London's Kings Cross Railroad Station.

Kurt S. Adler ornament featuring the Nimbus Two Thousand.

Ford Anglia is the name of the flying car that Harry and Ron used to get to Hogwarts at the beginning of their second year. The word "Anglia" is Latin for "England."

DIVINATION

The term **divination** refers to an attempt, by occult means, to investigate the unknown or predict the future. Professor Sibyll Trelawney at Hogwarts School of Witchcraft and Wizardry taught the students a variety of divination subjects, including the arts of palm reading, tea cup – or tea leaf – reading and crystal ball reading.

In the ancient practice of **tea leaf reading**, tea leaves that are left at the bottom of a cup are "read" by interpreting standard symbols and patterns that the reader sees in the leaves. Some common symbols include: apple = achievement; bell = news; harp = romance; ring = marriage. The term "tasseography" is also used to describe this branch of divination. The word "tass" means a small drinking cup or goblet.

Palm reading, or palmistry, is done by observing the lines and marks on the palm of someone's hand. Predictions of marriage, health, length of life and state of well-being are said to be made by interpreting the lines on the palm.

Reading **crystal balls** is also referred to as scrying – which means to gaze at crystals. Other reflective surfaces such as mirrors and pools or bowls of water are also used for scrying. The Mirror of Erised, in *Harry Potter and the Sorcerer's Stone*, and the Pensieve bowl from *Harry Potter and the Goblet of Fire* were both used like this.

CAVES AND SEA CREATURES

When Harry and Hagrid visited Gringotts in *Harry Potter and the Sorcerer's Stone*, Harry had asked the unanswered question about the difference between **stalactites** and **stalagmites**. Stalactites are icicle-shaped mineral deposits that hang from the roof of a cave and are formed by the evaporation of dripping water. Stalagmites are cone-shaped mineral deposits that build up on the floor of a cave and are formed by dripping water, usually from a stalactite above. Some people remember the difference this way: stalactites (spelled with a "c") grow from the "**c**"eiling and stalagmites (spelled with a "g") grow from the "**g**"round.

Stalactite formations in an actual cave in England.

Harry encountered **merpeople**, creatures with the tail of a fish and the head and upper body of a human, in *Harry Potter and the Goblet of Fire*. The prefix of the word merpeople – "mere" – means "lake or pond" in the Old Poetic language, "marsh" in the British dialect and has an obsolete definition of "the sea."

Homes

In the first chapters of *Harry Potter and the Sorcerer's Stone*, the reader is introduced to the boy who lived in a **cupboard** under the stairs at number four, Privet Drive, Little Whinging, in Surrey. As we read on, we begin to understand the horrendous conditions under which Harry lives in the Dursley household.

Ron Weasley, Harry's best friend, grew up in a house called the **Burrow**, with his parents and many siblings. Over several summers, Harry finds that Ron's house is the perfect place to escape from the Dursleys. After all, the word "burrow" is derived from a Middle English word which means "to take refuge."

Although regular people see just a "moldering old ruin" when they look at the Hogwarts School, in the world of witches and wizards, the school is a magnificent castle, similar to those commonly found across the British Isles. Many of these British castles are said to be inhabited by **castle ghosts**, each with its own dramatic tale. Windsor Castle is one of the most famous haunted castles in England, with frequent sightings of Queen Elizabeth I who died in 1603. Hogwarts is also home to many notorious ghosts.

Magic Words

Alchemy – an early form of chemistry that was studied during the Middle Ages, using magic and philosophy.

Astronomy – the scientific study of the universe including the stars and the planets. Professor Sinastra taught Astronomy class – scheduled on Wednesdays at midnight – to students at Hogwarts.

Basilisk – a lizard-like creature of medieval folklore whose stare can be fatal.

Boarhound – a large dog – usually a Great Dane – used to hunt wild boar.

Centaur – a Greek mythological creature with a man's head and the body and legs of a horse; also, a constellation of stars.

Fluffy, depicted here in a Hallmark door stop, is an interpretation of cerberus.

Cerberus – a three-headed dog guarding the gates of Hades in Greek and Roman mythology.

Dragon – a mythical monster that breathes fire and smoke and looks like a giant reptile with claws and a tail.

This ring from Tri-Star Merchandise features a dragon.

Elf – a small human-like creature known for its mischievous and magical behavior.

Gargoyle – guardian statues, usually in the shape of mythical creatures, found on castles and other buildings.

Ghost – the disembodied spirit of a dead person or animal.

Giant/Giantess – a man or woman of human form who has extreme size and strength.

Gnome – a small, misshapen dwarf-like creature who lives in the earth and protects hidden treasures.

Griffin – a mythical creature with the head, claws and wings of an eagle and the body and hind legs of a lion.

Magic Words

Hippogriff – a mythical creature that has the rear quarters of a horse but the head and wings of a griffin.

Mandrake – a poisonous plant with a thick root that resembles the human body. A magical form of this mystical plant is introduced to Harry and his classmates by their teacher of Herbology, Professor Sprout.

Phoenix – a bird that is said to be able to rise from its ashes after death and is a sign of immortality.

Potion – a drink thought to have magical powers. Professor Snape taught Potions class at Hogwarts School.

The "Potion Bottles" diary from Hallmark is the perfect place for you to write in your potion recipes and anything else.

Sirius – the "Dog Star;" the brightest star the sky; part of the constellation Canis Major.

Troll – a mythical creature who lives underground or in caves. A troll is usually either dwarf-like or giant in size and traditionally likes to eat people.

Unicorn – a mythical creature traditionally depicted as a white horse with a single horn growing from its forehead – said to have magical healing powers and good fortune.

Werewolf – humans that shift into the form of a wolf, usually during a full moon.

Witch – a woman skilled in supernatural arts such as divination, potions, spells, etc.

A typical wizards' hat can be seen in this Kurt S. Adler ornament.

Wizard – according to folklore, a man who is able to perform magic and brew potions.

If You Like Harry Potter, Try . . .

Here are some other great books to keep you reading until the next Harry Potter book is released. The name of the author is followed by the title and a short synopsis of the book.

For Ages 9 To 12

T.A. Barron, *The Lost Years Of Merlin* – In this saga about the childhood of the legendary wizard Merlin, the author chronicles the young wizard's life as he searches for his true identity.

John Bellairs, *The House With A Clock In Its Walls* – When Lewis is sent to live with his uncle after the death of his parents, he soon discovers that his uncle is a wizard and a clock hidden in the walls of their house is counting down to the world's end!

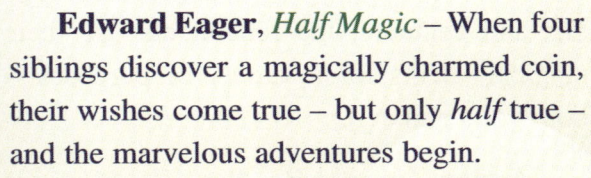

Edward Eager, *Half Magic* – When four siblings discover a magically charmed coin, their wishes come true – but only *half* true – and the marvelous adventures begin.

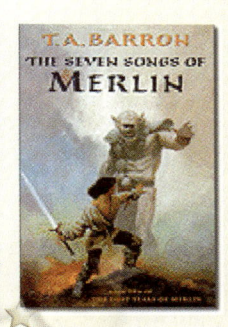

Eva Ibbotson, *The Secret Of Platform 13* – A prince is kidnapped from a magical island that is only accessible through a portal that opens every nine years. As the portal begins to reopen, a rescue crew sets out to bring back the prince.

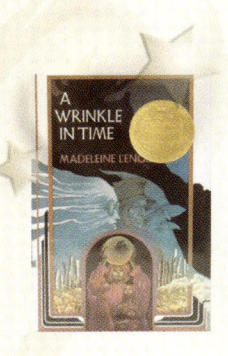

Madeleine L'Engle, *A Wrinkle In Time* – Elements of science fiction, fantasy and adventure combine in this 1963 Newbery Medal–winning story of children in search of their father.

Gail Carson Levine, *Ella Enchanted* – Cursed with a charm of "obedience" against her will, Ella comes to terms with the wishes of others and her own strong will in this Newbery Honor–winner.

C.S. Lewis, *The Chronicles Of Narnia* – This classic set of books explores the age-old struggle between good and evil as seen through the eyes of children.

For Ages 13 & Up

Piers Anthony, *The Magic Of Xanth Series* – In Xanth, the land of basilisks, dragons and centaurs, the inhabitants use their magical talents for a variety of purposes – both good and evil.

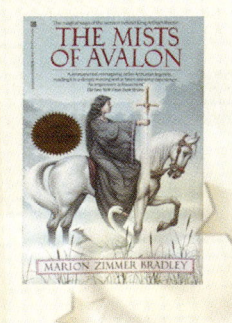

Marion Zimmer Bradley, *The Mists Of Avalon* – Told from a feminine point of view, the legend of King Arthur comes to life through the eyes of Morgaine, Arthur's half-sister, and Queen Gwynhefar.

If You Like Harry Potter, Try . . .

Diane Duane, *So You Want To Be A Wizard* – Two loners who are tormented by a group of bullies retreat to their school library and find answers to their problems in an instructional book on becoming a wizard.

David Eddings, *The Belgariad Series* and *The Mallorean Series* – A prophecy that must be fulfilled is the driving force behind these two series of books.

Philip Pullman, *The Golden Compass* – Young Lyra is orphaned and living at a university in Oxford when she discovers a plot to kidnap children and enters an alternate universe to try to save them.

J.R.R. Tolkien, *The Hobbit* and *The Lord Of The Rings* – Tolkien invents a world called "Middle-earth," featuring hobbits, wizards and other magical creatures.

T. H. White, *The Sword In The Stone* – A magician named Merlyn is serving as the mentor to a young boy named Wart who will grow up to be Arthur, the future king of England.

Patricia C. Wrede, *The Enchanted Forest Chronicles* – Princess Cimorene impulsively runs away from her structured life of royalty only to find herself in a fairy tale world made up of dragons and wizards.

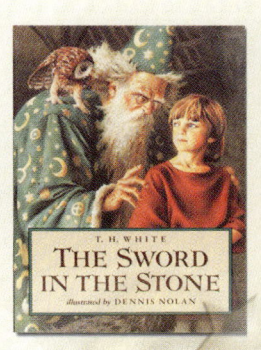

Take A Spellbinding Journey!

CollectorsQuest.com

If you love Harry Potter, CollectorsQuest is for you! Visit us today

- Keep up with the latest Harry Potter news!
- Meet other Harry Potter fans on our free Bulletin Board!
- Try your luck with our contests & giveaways!

Don't miss these other Enchanting Guides!

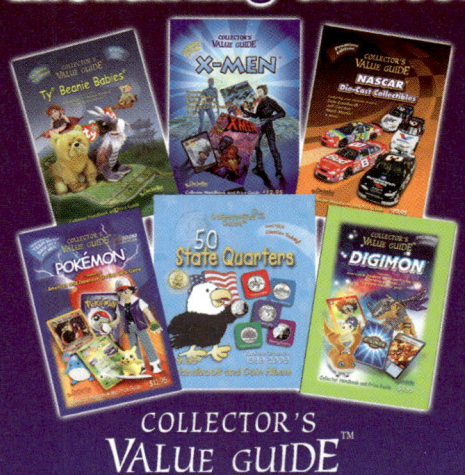

- Pokémon™
- Digimon™
- Hot Wheels®
- X-Men®
- Ty® Beanie Babies®
- Fifty State Quarters
- NASCAR®
- Jeff Gordon®
- Dale Earnhardt®
- Snow Buddies™
- Just the Right Shoe™
- And More...

COLLECTOR'S VALUE GUIDE™

CheckerBee PUBLISHING

We have 27 great titles in all - available in stores everywhere. Experience the magic today! To find out more, simply call:

800.746.3686 or visit CollectorsQuest.com